Patchwork Quilts for Kids You Love

Linda Seward

Sterling Publishing Co., Inc.   New York

For the man I love.

EDITED BY VILMA LIACOURAS CHANTILES

Library of Congress Cataloging in Publication Data

Seward, Linda.
   Patchwork quilts for kids you love.

   Includes index.
   1. Quilting.   2. Patchwork.   I. Title.
TT835.S46   1985   746.9′7   85-9907
ISBN 0-8069-5728-X
ISBN 0-8069-6248-8 (pbk.)

Copyright © 1985 by Linda Seward
Published by Sterling Publishing Co., Inc.
Two Park Avenue, New York, N.Y. 10016
Distributed in Australia by Capricorn Book Co. Pty. Ltd.
Unit 5C1 Lincoln St., Lane Cove, N.S.W. 2066
Distributed in the United Kingdom by Blandford Press
Link House, West Street, Poole, Dorset BH15 1LL, England
Distributed in Canada by Oak Tree Press Ltd.
% Canadian Manda Group, P.O. Box 920, Station U
Toronto, Ontario, Canada M8Z 5P9
Manufactured in the United States of America
All rights reserved

Contents

ACKNOWLEDGMENTS

I would like to thank the following people who so willingly contributed their efforts to help me prepare this book:

My friend, Jean Kubitz, who pieced and quilted the By the Sea quilt.

My mother, Evelyn Macho, who did all the quilting and handwork on the Flowers quilt.

My brother, Jim Macho, and his wife, Rosie, who helped me with some of the photography one snowy afternoon.

My friend, Janette Aiello, who drew most of the illustrations for the chapter, Making a Quilt.

My editor, Vilma Chantiles, who pulled everything together.

My husband, Robert, who cooked, cleaned, arranged quilt blocks, drafted some templates and generally encouraged me to finish.

Introduction

*P*atchwork Quilts for Kids You Love has been designed and written for adult quilters who love children, want to give a memorable handmade gift to a favorite child and don't want to spend too much time making the gift.

Children love to snuggle under a quilt—especially one that has been created just for them. Boys and girls delight in the bright colors and puffy textures that characterize a quilt and it is quite pleasurable to create one for such an appreciative audience!

Making a quilt for a child, therefore, is a satisfying experience. A quilt is fun to design, quick to make and rewarding to give. The process of making a quilt can become more relaxing when you make one for a child, and the piecing is easier when you feel relaxed about it. Experiment with playful patterns and imaginative hues when making a child's quilt. You may find you are a more creative quilter than you dreamed possible.

Quilting requires patience, persistence and, usually, a considerable amount of time. But imagine how lovely it would be to decide to make a quilt and finish it within a few days or weeks! This is the advantage of making quilts for children: each project is relatively small, which means it requires less piecing and quilting than an adult quilt.

The piecing (patchwork) for a quilt can be done in a week during your spare time and then quilted at leisure in a week or two. Because of the conveniently small size, it can be carried with you to do the handwork wherever you are and whenever you can. I did all the hand-quilting on the Bright Hopes quilt in airports and on airplanes. The quilt sparked interesting conversations and was a very pleasant way to spend my time at 30,000 feet! Also, because of the quilt size, less fabric and batting are required, considerably reducing the cost. Therefore, a smaller monetary investment is needed.

Making a quilt for a child is a terrific way to satisfy your urge to make a unique quilt. Use all the ideas you've always wanted to use in a large quilt but felt were out of place for such a traditional project. When you give the gift—a quilt you make—both the child and mother will appreciate and treasure it.

How to Use This Book

This book contains 130 designs specially related to children and their mothers. Keep in mind that a gift for a newborn infant is a gift for the mother, too!

The quilt designs are arranged into eight chapters: By the Sea; Outdoor Fun; Snips & Snails & Puppy Dog Tails; Flowers; Sugar & Spice & All Things Nice; Country Fun; Toys & Games; Bright Hopes. Some of the designs are traditional, but these are mixed in with a selection of new designs that have never before been published.

The way to use this book is simple. *All of the blocks are eight inches square*, which means that any block in the book can be used interchangeably with the others. First, decide how large you want to make your quilt. There are ten different quilt styles from which to choose (pages 24–30). Based on the quilt style you select, determine how many designs you will need to make by looking at the Requirements for that quilt, in the chapter, Styling a Quilt.

Then begin browsing through the book to select the designs. It would be easy and interesting to base your quilt on a theme, such as the sea, flowers or a theme you know is a favorite of your loved child. If you are making a quilt for a newborn or an expected baby, it would be best to make your selection from the Toys & Games and Bright Hopes chapters of the book; or mix together designs from all the sections.

I recommend that you create a sampler quilt with many motifs for your child. If you prefer, it is perfectly acceptable to repeat your favorite block many times to create an allover pattern. Children delight in sensory experiences, and the different colors and combinations of shapes and patterns in a sampler quilt are more appealing to them than the repetition of one design.

When the child is old enough, you can have even more fun taking this one step further by teaching him or her the names of the blocks you made on the quilt. Then you can explain why you chose those designs. Encourage the child to re-create favorite blocks, using felt or scrap fabrics, or by drawing the blocks and then coloring the drawings. Your encouragement will stimulate creativity and an awareness of the many possible color combinations in geometric patterns. It may also encourage potential quilters to take up the needle at an early age!

Precautions

One basic consideration when making a quilt for a child needs no explanation: the quilt should be washable. Prewash all the fabrics before you even begin to think about using them. Wash the fabrics in the very hottest water and hang them to dry (tangling in a clothes dryer can twist the fabrics off-grain). If there is any evidence that the fabric is not colorfast (the colors will bleed), wash the fabric again; or soak it in a solution of three parts cold water and one part white vinegar. Rinse the fabric and spread it on a white towel while wet. If there is still evidence of color bleeding, discard the fabric and select another. It is better to make this effort in the beginning than to experience the horror of washing a finished quilt only to find that it has been ruined by bleeding fabrics.

To ensure washability, use polyester batting in your quilt and do not leave an area unquilted more than two inches square. This method will prevent unsightly lumps in the batting when the quilt is washed.

Careful youngsters will have no trouble taking care of a pretty pink-and-white quilt, but children with soiled fingers will be very hard on their quilts. You are making the quilts to be used, so try to select a predominance of colors and patterns that will not easily show the dirt; this care in choosing colors will avoid excessive washing of the finished quilt.

Metric Equivalency Chart

MM—Millimetres   CM—Centimetres

INCHES TO MILLIMETRES AND CENTIMETRES

INCHES	MM	CM	INCHES	CM	INCHES	CM
$\frac{1}{8}$	3	0.3	9	22.9	30	76.2
$\frac{1}{4}$	6	0.6	10	25.4	31	78.7
$\frac{3}{8}$	10	1.0	11	27.9	32	81.3
$\frac{1}{2}$	13	1.3	12	30.5	33	83.8
$\frac{5}{8}$	16	1.6	13	33.0	34	86.4
$\frac{3}{4}$	19	1.9	14	35.6	35	88.9
$\frac{7}{8}$	22	2.2	15	38.1	36	91.4
1	25	2.5	16	40.6	37	94.0
$1\frac{1}{4}$	32	3.2	17	43.2	38	96.5
$1\frac{1}{2}$	38	3.8	18	45.7	39	99.1
$1\frac{3}{4}$	44	4.4	19	48.3	40	101.6
2	51	5.1	20	50.8	41	104.1
$2\frac{1}{2}$	64	6.4	21	53.3	42	106.7
3	76	7.6	22	55.9	43	109.2
$3\frac{1}{2}$	89	8.9	23	58.4	44	111.8
4	102	10.2	24	61.0	45	114.3
$4\frac{1}{2}$	114	11.4	25	63.5	46	116.8
5	127	12.7	26	66.0	47	119.4
6	152	15.2	27	68.6	48	121.9
7	178	17.8	28	71.1	49	124.5
8	203	20.3	29	73.7	50	127.0

YARDS TO METRES

YARDS	METRES	YARDS	METRES	YARDS	METRES	YARDS	METRES	YARDS	METRES
$\frac{1}{8}$	0.11	$2\frac{1}{8}$	1.94	$4\frac{1}{8}$	3.77	$6\frac{1}{8}$	5.60	$8\frac{1}{8}$	7.43
$\frac{1}{4}$	0.23	$2\frac{1}{4}$	2.06	$4\frac{1}{4}$	3.89	$6\frac{1}{4}$	5.72	$8\frac{1}{4}$	7.54
$\frac{3}{8}$	0.34	$2\frac{3}{8}$	2.17	$4\frac{3}{8}$	4.00	$6\frac{3}{8}$	5.83	$8\frac{3}{8}$	7.66
$\frac{1}{2}$	0.46	$2\frac{1}{2}$	2.29	$4\frac{1}{2}$	4.11	$6\frac{1}{2}$	5.94	$8\frac{1}{2}$	7.77
$\frac{5}{8}$	0.57	$2\frac{5}{8}$	2.40	$4\frac{5}{8}$	4.23	$6\frac{5}{8}$	6.06	$8\frac{5}{8}$	7.89
$\frac{3}{4}$	0.69	$2\frac{3}{4}$	2.51	$4\frac{3}{4}$	4.34	$6\frac{3}{4}$	6.17	$8\frac{3}{4}$	8.00
$\frac{7}{8}$	0.80	$2\frac{7}{8}$	2.63	$4\frac{7}{8}$	4.46	$6\frac{7}{8}$	6.29	$8\frac{7}{8}$	8.12
1	0.91	3	2.74	5	4.57	7	6.40	9	8.23
$1\frac{1}{8}$	1.03	$3\frac{1}{8}$	2.86	$5\frac{1}{8}$	4.69	$7\frac{1}{8}$	6.52	$9\frac{1}{8}$	8.34
$1\frac{1}{4}$	1.14	$3\frac{1}{4}$	2.97	$5\frac{1}{4}$	4.80	$7\frac{1}{4}$	6.63	$9\frac{1}{4}$	8.46
$1\frac{3}{8}$	1.26	$3\frac{3}{8}$	3.09	$5\frac{3}{8}$	4.91	$7\frac{3}{8}$	6.74	$9\frac{3}{8}$	8.57
$1\frac{1}{2}$	1.37	$3\frac{1}{2}$	3.20	$5\frac{1}{2}$	5.03	$7\frac{1}{2}$	6.86	$9\frac{1}{2}$	8.69
$1\frac{5}{8}$	1.49	$3\frac{5}{8}$	3.31	$5\frac{5}{8}$	5.14	$7\frac{5}{8}$	6.97	$9\frac{5}{8}$	8.80
$1\frac{3}{4}$	1.60	$3\frac{3}{4}$	3.43	$5\frac{3}{4}$	5.26	$7\frac{3}{4}$	7.09	$9\frac{3}{4}$	8.92
$1\frac{7}{8}$	1.71	$3\frac{7}{8}$	3.54	$5\frac{7}{8}$	5.37	$7\frac{7}{8}$	7.20	$9\frac{7}{8}$	9.03
2	1.83	4	3.66	6	5.49	8	7.32	10	9.14

Making a Quilt

Choose a quilt style from those illustrated on pages 24–30; or design one of your own. If you use your own quilt style, make sure that each pieced block in your creation is eight inches square so that you can use the templates given in this book. Determine how many blocks you'll need. Then have fun looking through the book to select the perfect designs for your quilt. Try to include a variety of geometric shapes to add interest to the finished project.

Selecting Fabrics, Threads & Bindings

Each block design is accompanied by a screened illustration, an assembly diagram and a list of templates that tells you how many pieces are needed and their suggested color value (degree of light or dark): white, light, bright, medium, dark. Follow exactly the block lists, diagrams and illustrations; or experiment with the placement of colors to create your own interpretation of each design. (*Note:* Whenever a value is followed by a Roman numeral—for example, light I, light II—it means that two different fabrics of a similar value are required.)

It is best to use five or six different fabrics in a quilt. For a more vibrant and colorful effect, use as many colors as you feel comfortable with (I used eight colors in the Toys & Games quilt (color photo, page A1). When you decide how many you will use, make sure that the number of fabrics corresponds with the number of values in the designs you have chosen.

Fabrics woven from 100-percent cotton threads are best for quiltmaking, although fabrics with some polyester content can be used. Don't use anything with less than 70-percent cotton, however. Select fabrics with highly contrasting values. Unorthodox combinations are fine and fun to use—especially in a child's quilt. Select an attractive interplay of solid fabrics (or fabrics with a tiny allover print), fabrics with a medium-scale print and at least one with a large-scale print. Try to buy all fabrics for your quilt at the same time. You can see how colors and patterns work with one another while they are still on the bolt. Matching fabrics from small scraps is very difficult and quite often doesn't work when you take the new selections home.

If in doubt about yardages, always buy *more* fabric than you think you'll need. Dye lots vary considerably; often, by the time you realize that you'll need more fabric, it may be too late to find the same dye lot. The fabric yardages listed with the Requirements for each quilt style are exact and assume your cutting is precise. If you're not sure about the accuracy of your cutting, buy a little more fabric—you can always use the leftover pieces in some future creation.

When you are satisfied with your fabric choices, buy your sewing thread—an unobtrusive color that will blend with all the fabrics. Again, all-cotton thread is best, although cotton wrapped around a polyester core is fine.

At this time, it is probably best to also buy the fabric for the stripping (if needed), border, back and binding. Do not use commercially made bindings; you'll never get a perfect match and, most likely, the binding fabric will be inferior to your selection for the quilt you are making. Preferably, make the binding from one of the fabrics used in the blocks or stripping; or make the back lining about one and one-half inches larger all around and use the excess fabric to self-bind the quilt. It is important to plan and prepare for the binding when selecting fabrics. See more about bindings on pages 20–22.

Washing & Straightening

Prewash all fabrics to be used in your quilt. Clip into the selvages (finished edges) at two-inch intervals to accommodate shrinkage before putting the fabrics in the washing machine. Read Precautions (page 9) for more details of this procedure. If possible, iron the fabrics while they are slightly damp; the dampness makes it easier to remove all the wrinkles.

Check the grain. The crosswise and lengthwise threads of the fabric should be exactly perpendicular to each other. If they aren't perpendicular (and this is better when done with two pairs of hands), grasp the four corners of the fabric and pull diagonally from opposite corners simultaneously to straighten the grain. Repeat this pulling alternately from opposite corners until the threads are perpendicular to one another.

Prepare the fabrics for cutting as follows: accurately cut off the selvages. To do this, measure an even distance from each finished edge (selvages are usually a quarter inch but can be as wide as a half inch); draw a cutting line with a pencil and ruler. Cut away the selvages along the pencil line. Next, using a triangle and a ruler, draw a line across the fabric that is exactly perpendicular to the cut edge (Fig. 1). Cut away any excess fabric beyond this line. You are

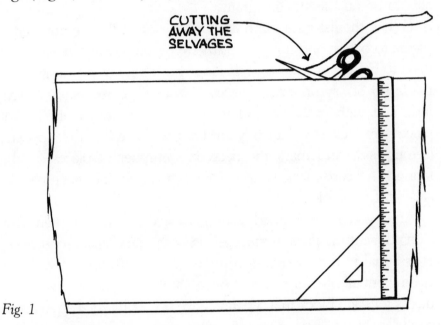

Fig. 1

now ready to make your templates, mark your fabric and cut out your pieces.

Making Templates & Cutting the Pieces

Using tracing paper and a pencil, trace the templates for the designs you have chosen. Mark each tracing with the name of the design, the letter of the template (the letter "I" is not used for templates in this book) and the value(s) of the fabric(s) from which it should be cut.

Glue the tracing to medium-weight cardboard or plastic; allow the glue to dry. Cut out each template using an X-acto knife or other cutting blade. For straight lines, use a straight metal edge to guide the knife.

The edge of the template is the sewing line; therefore, a quarter-inch seam allowance *must be added* when marking the templates on the fabric. The best way to do this is by drawing a

Fig. 2

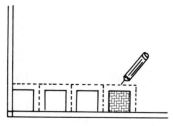

Fig. 3

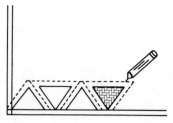

Fig. 4

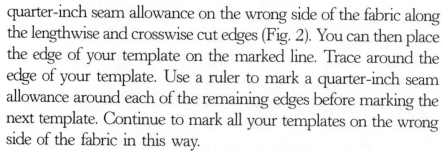

quarter-inch seam allowance on the wrong side of the fabric along the lengthwise and crosswise cut edges (Fig. 2). You can then place the edge of your template on the marked line. Trace around the edge of your template. Use a ruler to mark a quarter-inch seam allowance around each of the remaining edges before marking the next template. Continue to mark all your templates on the wrong side of the fabric in this way.

To avoid waste and conserve fabric, mark your pieces so they can be cut along a mutual edge (Fig. 3 and Fig. 4). As a rule, the longest edge of any template should be placed on the straight (lengthwise) grain of the fabric. *All* edges of squares and rectangles should be on the straight grain.

Follow the list given with each block design for the number of pieces to be cut and how to cut them. Symmetrical pieces do not need to be flipped over or "reversed," but many of the designs are made up of asymmetrical pieces; this need to reverse is always indicated with each list. Where the list indicates a number of pieces are "reversed," turn your template over to the opposite (wrong) side and mark the necessary number of pieces on the fabric. You can check your work by studying the assembly diagram of your block.

After you have marked your pieces, carefully cut them out along the cutting lines. *Accuracy*—in both marking and cutting—is essential to the successful completion of each block. If you are cutting out all of your pieces at once, carefully gather and keep the pieces for each block in a separate envelope or plastic bag to avoid confusion when sewing time arrives.

Sewing the Pieces: Patchwork

I assume that you will use a sewing machine to sew the pieces or patches for the quilt top, although it is perfectly acceptable (though much slower) to do the piecing by hand.

Each block design is accompanied by complete piecing instructions. Most blocks are assembled in sub-units (squares, triangles, strips) that are then joined to complete the design.

When sewing pieces together, match the raw edges carefully, pinning them together at each end if necessary (Fig. 5). Sew the pieces together in chains to save time (Fig. 6). Always press the seams to one side, preferably towards the darker fabric (Fig. 7).

When sewing sub-units together, carefully match the seams before you sew, pinning the pieces at crucial points (Fig. 8). When

Fig. 5

matching seams, it is best to press seam allowances in opposite directions.

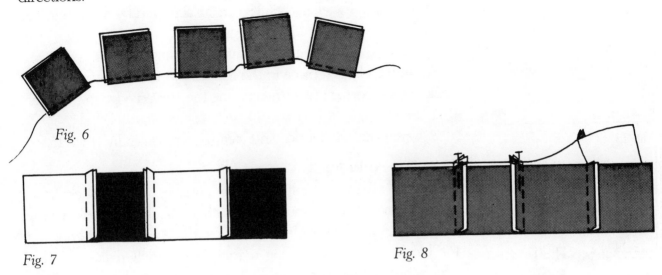

Fig. 6

Fig. 7

Fig. 8

HOW TO INSET

Sometimes, pieces of a design must be inset into one another. While this procedure is slightly tricky at first, it is possible to get perfect corners every time by using the following method:

1. A triangular or square piece is inset into two other pieces that are sewn together to form an angle (Fig. 9). When sewing those pieces together, end your stitching a quarter inch away from the edge to be inset (shown by the dot in the diagram).

2. Pin the piece to be inset along one edge of the angle (Fig. 10) and stitch from the middle (dot) to the edge (in the direction of the arrow).

3. Folding the excess fabric out of the way, pin the unsewn edges together and stitch from the central point to the outer edge (Fig. 11).

4. Open out the fabrics and carefully steam-press (Fig. 12). If you notice any puckers at the corner, you can usually eliminate them by removing a stitch from one of the seams just sewn.

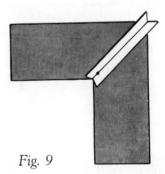

Fig. 9

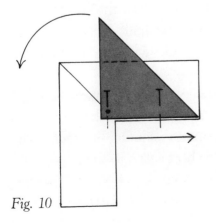

Fig. 10

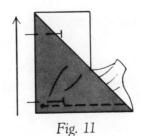

Fig. 11

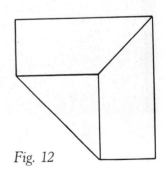

Fig. 12

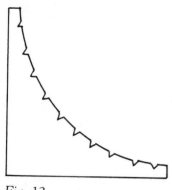

Fig. 13

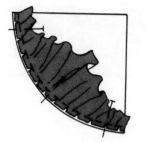

Fig. 14

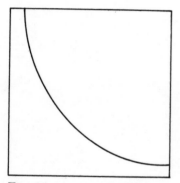

Fig. 15

SEWING CURVES

Curved edges are time-consuming to sew, but quite rewarding when finished. Excellent results can be achieved by following this procedure:

1. Clip the curve of the concave piece (Fig. 13).
2. Pin the clipped piece to the convex piece, matching the right angles at the corners first, then easing the curved edge to fit; stitch (Fig. 14).
3. Open out the fabrics and steam-press carefully (Fig. 15).

HOW TO APPLIQUÉ

"Appliqué" means to apply to a larger surface, or in this technique, to apply one piece of fabric over another. While this book mainly features patchwork (or pieced) designs, there are some sections of the block where appliquéing a tricky piece will make a design simple rather than challenging. The idea is to make the appliqué look like part of the patchwork, and to achieve this look hand-appliqué is recommended.

When cutting out the piece for each appliqué, be sure to add a quarter-inch seam allowance around the edges. Machine-stitch along the sewing line, using tiny stitches. Press the seam allowance to the wrong side, clipping into the seam allowance, where necessary, for ease; the machine stitches should be pressed just below the edge so they are not visible. Baste the seam allowance in place, if desired.

Place the pressed appliqué in its correct position on your patchwork. Slip-stitch in place using tiny invisible stitches. Backstitch at the end to secure your thread.

Stripping

Stripping or latticework—the horizontal and vertical strips of fabric used to join together the blocks of the quilt top—can be used to set off blocks to their best advantage. Cut the strips to the size indicated in the Requirements for the quilt style you have chosen. Then join together the pieced blocks with the short strips; press carefully.

For the long strips, using a pencil and ruler, mark off the position of the seams to which the strip will be attached. (This is where stripping will help you to maintain accuracy in your quilt top.) Then sew the pieced blocks and short strips to the long strip, matching your markings to the seams. For example, if you are making the 6-Block Quilt (page 25), mark off a quarter inch for the outer seam allowance; measure eight inches and mark off the edge of the first block. Mark off two inches for the short strip, then mark off another eight inches for the second block. Finally, mark off a quarter inch for the remaining seam allowance.

When sewing the stripping in place, match up your markings *accurately* to the seams—don't be tempted to trim off excess from the end of the stripping to make it come out even! Press carefully when finished.

Continue joining the pieced blocks with the stripping until the quilt top is completely assembled.

Sewing the Border

The border is the last step to complete the quilt top. If you are making a patchwork border, sew the pieces together before attaching the complete border to the quilt top.

When sewing the border to the quilt top, mark the position of the seams and stripping along the edge as you did for the long stripping. Sew the border in place, matching the markings to the seams, and beginning and ending a quarter inch from the outer edge of the quilt top. (*Note:* The border will be longer than the quilt top by its width at each corner.)

When all four borders are sewn to the edges of the quilt top, mitre the corners as follows: turn the quilt top to the wrong side. Fold the raw ends of adjacent border strips back on themselves to form a 45° angle (Fig. 16). Press. Pin and sew the edges together, matching the creases formed by the pressing. Check the right side to make sure that the corner is perfect, with no puckers. If there are puckers, you can usually correct them by removing one of the stitches (as in step 4 of How to Inset). If the corner is perfect (Fig. 17), trim away the excess seam allowance, leaving a quarter-inch seam allowance. Press carefully.

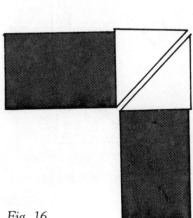

Fig. 16

Fig. 17

Batting

Batting is available made from polyester, cotton or wool. For washability, it is probably best to choose a polyester batting for your child's quilt. Select a thin batting rather than a thicker one to keep the puffiness in scale with the size of the quilt; it is also easier to quilt through a thinner batting.

Assembling the Quilt

A quilt is actually like a sandwich, with the batting as the filling and the top and back as the bread. To make the sandwich, you'll need a large flat surface, such as a large worktable or the floor.

Iron the back very well; tape it to the work surface, wrong side up, with the grain straight and all corners making 90° angles. Carefully place the batting over the lining, matching all outside edges. If you must piece the batting, butt the edges and baste them together with large cross stitches.

Press the quilt top carefully—this will be the last time it will be ironed, so make the pressing a good one. Trim away any uneven seams on the back, or any ravelled edges. When you are satisfied, set the quilt top, right side up, over the batting to match the outside edges of the layers.

Baste together the three layers quite thoroughly: first baste diagonally from the middle to each corner, then crosswise and lengthwise (Fig. 18). If you are using a quilting frame, put the quilt

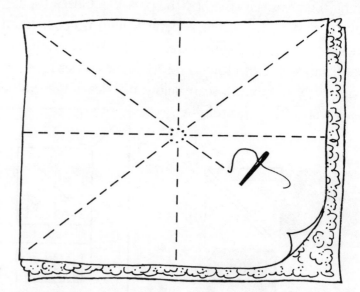

Fig. 18

into the frame. If quilting with a hoop, add some additional basting (concentric squares) for extra safety.

You are now ready to quilt.

How to Quilt

You'll need a quilting or "between" needle, size 7 through 10 (10 is the smallest); an 8 needle is a good size for most quilters. A thimble for the middle finger of your sewing hand is essential as is strong and mercerized 100-percent cotton quilting thread. Some quilters like to use a second thimble on the index finger of the hand under the quilt; this is optional.

To begin, cut an 18-inch length of quilting thread; thread your needle and knot the end of the thread. Run the needle and thread through the quilt top and some of the batting, pulling the knot beneath the surface of the quilt top (it usually makes a satisfying "popping" sound) and burying it in the batting (Fig. 19).

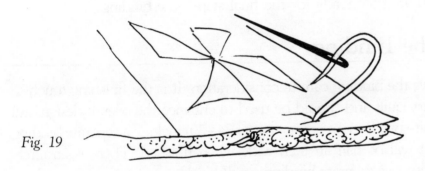

Fig. 19

The quilting stitch is basically a running stitch. Hold the index finger of your left hand (for right-handed quilters) or right hand (for left-handed quilters) beneath the quilt just below the spot where you wish to make your stitches. Try to achieve a smooth rhythm, rocking your needle from the surface of the quilt to the back, then returning it again to the surface. Try to make three to four stitches at a time. Fig. 20 shows how to use the thimble to

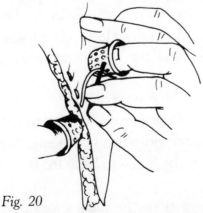

Fig. 20

help push the needle through the fabric; the illustration also shows how the finger beneath pushes against the quilt to compress the batting, making it easier to take several stitches at a time.

Don't panic if your stitches look larger than you think they should—an *even line* of stitches is the important procedure, not the size of the stitches. The more you quilt, the smaller your stitches will become, but in the beginning, concentrate on making the stitches the same length on the quilt top and on the back.

Suggestions for how to quilt each block are given at the end of each set of piecing instructions. The stripping and borders should also be quilted in a pattern that is complementary to the overall quilt design. For quilting ideas, see Fig. 21 and also the finished quilts shown in color (pages A–H).

If you are using a hoop, baste strips of fabric, six to twelve inches wide, to the edges of the quilt so that the quilt can be held in the hoop when you are quilting the border.

When the quilting is finished, remove your basting stitches. You are now ready for the final step—the binding.

The Binding

Give the binding careful consideration. It is the finishing touch to every quilt and should be used to enhance the overall design. All quilt-style Requirements (pages 24–30) include a separate binding that will be half an inch wide when finished. There is an alternative to a separate binding—self-binding—mentioned in Selecting Fabrics, Threads & Bindings.

SELF-BINDING
Self-binding is a quick and easy way to finish a quilt. It is not always recommended when the back is made from the same fabric as the border because it can make the edges of the quilt seem to fade away, particularly if the pieced blocks are very strong. For example, look at the Toys & Games quilt (page A1). The vibrant binding is essential here in order to balance the bright colors in the blocks. Now turn to the Bright Hopes quilt (page B1). The mood of the quilt is quiet and the self-border enhances the tranquil effect.

If you decide to self-bind your quilt, mark and cut an extra inch all around the edge of the fabric for the back; this will add two inches to the length and width measurements. Arrange the batting and top carefully over the lining to leave the inch-wide border free around the edges.

After the quilting is done, to make a folded edge, finger-press the edges of the back half an inch inwards to the wrong side of the fabric. Then wrap the back towards the quilt top, covering the

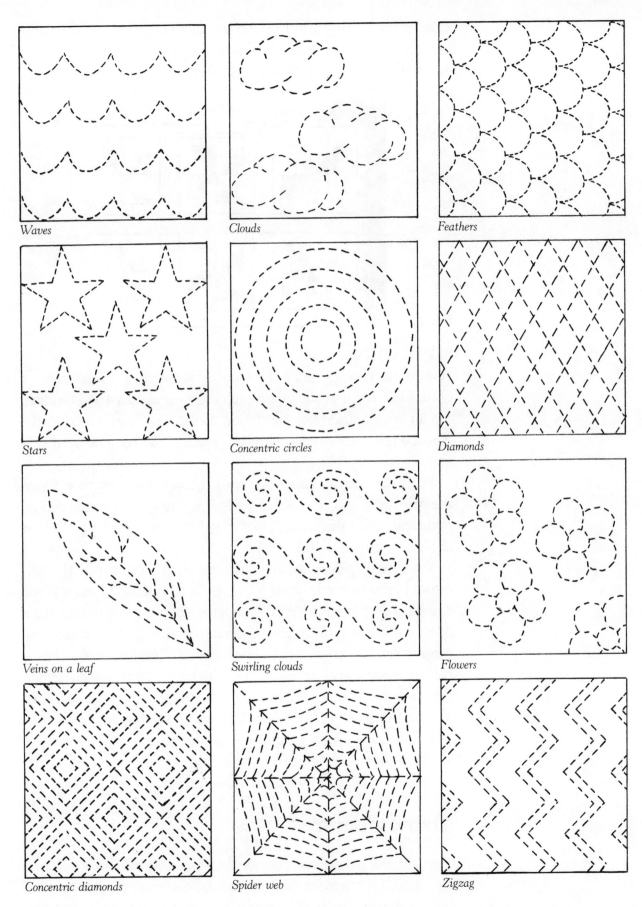

Waves

Clouds

Feathers

Stars

Concentric circles

Diamonds

Veins on a leaf

Swirling clouds

Flowers

Concentric diamonds

Spider web

Zigzag

Fig. 21

edges of the batting and top. Pin the folded edge to the quilt top (Fig. 22). Slip-stitch invisibly the folded edge of the back to the quilt top. Mitre the corners and remove all pins when finished.

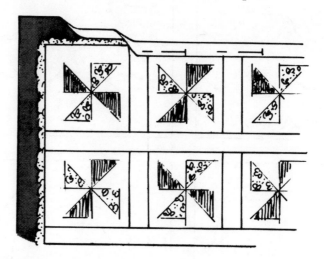

Fig. 22

SEPARATE BINDING

A separate binding adds a certain amount of freedom to your choice, but it does take a bit more time to sew than a self-binding.

Cut your chosen binding fabric to the length indicated in the Requirements for your quilt style, piecing the binding as necessary.

Press the strip in half lengthwise, wrong sides together. Open the strip and press one long raw edge exactly to the pressed central fold, again with the wrong sides together; this folded edge is later slip-stitched to the quilt back.

With right sides together and raw edges even, pin the unpressed edge of the binding to the quilt top, allowing extra fabric at each corner for mitring. To stitch together: start your stitching a quarter inch away from the beginning of the binding to facilitate turning that raw edge under, thus forming a finished edge. Make a half-inch seam and turn stitching sharply at each corner. When you have bound the whole quilt, trim away any excess binding. You do not have to fold under the end of the binding; just make sure it overlaps the beginning by about half an inch.

Wrap the pressed edge of the binding over the raw edges of the quilt to the back; slip-stitch invisibly, and mitre the corners.

Your Signature

Your gift will have greater personal and historic value if it is signed and dated. Embroider your name and the date on the front or back of the quilt with embroidery floss or sign your name and date on the back with indelible ink.

Styling a Quilt

Patchwork quilting offers myriad creative possibilities—from deciding on the fabric to choosing the block designs and, ultimately, the quilting patterns. These many choices, however, are governed by the size and style of the quilt you wish to make. This section offers ten different quilt styles from which to choose. Study them carefully, then select a style that fits in best with your plans.

A smaller quilt requires less time, effort and cost to make. The 4-Block Quilt is an ideal choice as a gift for a friend who is about to have a baby; it is easily completed in a very short time, yet will be treasured much more than a ready-made baby blanket. The 6-Block Quilt and 6-Block Quilt with Fancy Border also are delightful gifts for expectant parents but take a bit more time to make.

If you are creating a quilt for a very special child, you may want to put more time into it—perhaps by making a larger quilt that can be used for many years as the child grows. Choose from the 7-, 9- and 12-Block Quilt styles. Older children and teenagers will value a quilt even more than toddlers, especially if they can be involved in selecting fabrics, colors and designs. For older children, make the 15- or 24-Block Quilts.

If you want to save time, quilts made with many blocks can be completed quickly by alternating the patchwork blocks with plain ones. The plain blocks can be later livened with a special quilting pattern. The Flowers quilt (page D1), for example, is actually made from only eight pieced blocks, greatly reducing the time needed to make the quilt top. It is very important to select the fabric for the plain blocks with great care, however. In the Flowers quilt, the lovely trellis effect of the fabric print made it a compatible choice to set off the patchwork flower blocks. The trellis design later served as an excellent guide for the diagonal quilting worked on the plain blocks and the border. If you make a quilt with very bold colors and dominant geometric shapes, it would be wise to select a harmonizing solid color fabric for the plain blocks. In the planning stage, your eye will tell you whether the plain blocks enhance or detract from the patchwork.

The size of a quilt can be enlarged without too much effort by adding a border around the individual blocks or by adding extra borders around the edge of the quilt. These techniques merely involve straight, simple sewing, and add interest to the quilt in addition to making it slightly larger. Borders around each block act as "frames," making each design stand out to its best advantage; look at the By the Sea quilt (page F1) to observe the effect of framed blocks. A fancy border can be included to accentuate a favorite fabric when it is used as a narrow stripe around the edge of a quilt.

With all these factors in mind, select a style best suited to the child for which the quilt is intended. After you have made your selection, follow the Requirements given with that style to determine how much fabric you'll need. Then enjoy the fun of choosing colors, fabrics and block designs.

4-Block Quilt

Requirements

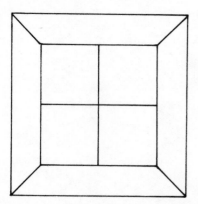

	MEASUREMENTS	NUMBER	YARDAGE
Finished Size	24 × 24″		
Blocks	8″ square	4	$\frac{3}{8}$ yard each of 4 fabrics
Stripping	none		
Border	4″ wide $4\frac{1}{4} \times 24\frac{1}{2}$″	4	$\frac{1}{2}$ yard
Back	25 × 25″	1	$\frac{3}{4}$ yard
Binding	2 × 100″	1	$\frac{1}{4}$ yard

6-Block Quilt

(Style of Bright Hopes quilt; color photo, page B1.)

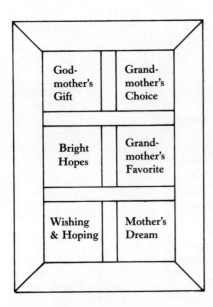

Requirements

	MEASUREMENTS	NUMBER	YARDAGE
Finished Size	26 × 36″		
Blocks	8″ square	6	$\frac{3}{8}$ yard each of 5 fabrics
Stripping	2″ wide		$\frac{1}{4}$ yard
Horizontal	2½ × 18½″	2	
Vertical	2½ × 8½″	3	
Border	4″ wide		$\frac{5}{8}$ yard
Horizontal	4½ × 26½″	2	
Vertical	4½ × 36½″	2	
Back	27 × 37″	1	1 yard
Binding	2 × 128″	1	$\frac{1}{4}$ yard

The block diagram labels (top to bottom, left to right): God-mother's Gift, Grand-mother's Choice, Bright Hopes, Grand-mother's Favorite, Wishing & Hoping, Mother's Dream.

6-Block Quilt with Fancy Border

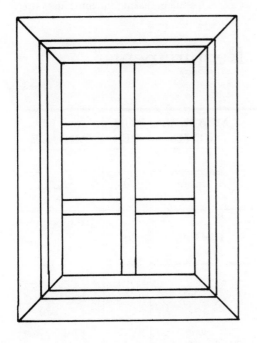

Requirements

	MEASUREMENTS	NUMBER	YARDAGE
Finished Size	30 × 40″		
Blocks	8″ square	6	$\frac{3}{8}$ yard each of 5 fabrics
Stripping	2″ wide		$\frac{1}{4}$ yard
Horizontal	2½ × 8½″	4	
Vertical	2½ × 28½″	1	
Inner Border	2″ wide		$\frac{3}{8}$ yard
Horizontal	2½ × 22½″	2	
Vertical	2½ × 32½″	2	
Middle Border	1″ wide		$\frac{1}{4}$ yard
Horizontal	1½ × 24½″	2	
Vertical	1½ × 34½″	2	
Outer Border	3″ wide		$\frac{1}{2}$ yard
Horizontal	3½ × 30½″	2	
Vertical	3½ × 40½″	2	
Back	31 × 41″	1	1 yard
Binding	2 × 144″	1	$\frac{1}{2}$ yard

7-Block Quilt

Requirements

	MEASURE-MENTS	NUM-BER	YARDAGE
Finished Size	$40 \times 51\frac{1}{8}''$		
Blocks			
Pieced squares	8″ square	7	$\frac{3}{8}$ yard each of 5 fabrics
Plain triangles	$8 \times 8 \times 11\frac{3}{8}''$	6	
Plain triangles	$6 \times 6 \times 8\frac{1}{2}''$	4	$\frac{1}{2}$ yard
Stripping	2″ wide		$\frac{3}{8}$ yard
A	$2\frac{1}{2} \times 8\frac{1}{2}''$	12	
B	$2\frac{1}{2} \times 20\frac{1}{2}''$	2	
C	$2\frac{1}{2} \times 40\frac{1}{2}''$	2	
Inner Border	$2\frac{1}{2}''$ wide		$\frac{3}{8}$ yard
Horizontal	$3 \times 31\frac{1}{2}''$	2	
Vertical	$3 \times 43\frac{5}{8}''$	2	
Middle Border	$1\frac{1}{2}''$ wide		$1\frac{1}{8}$ yards
Horizontal	$2 \times 34\frac{1}{2}''$	2	
Vertical	$2 \times 46\frac{5}{8}''$	2	
Outer Border	3″ wide		$1\frac{1}{4}$ yards
Horizontal	$3\frac{1}{2} \times 40\frac{1}{2}''$	2	
Vertical	$3\frac{1}{2} \times 52\frac{1}{8}''$	2	
Back	$41 \times 53\frac{1}{8}''$	1	$1\frac{1}{4}$ yards
Binding	$2 \times 188\frac{1}{4}''$	1	$\frac{1}{2}$ yard

Note: Buy only $1\frac{1}{4}$ yards if you are making the inner and outer borders from the same fabric.

Fancy 9-Block Quilt

(Style of By the Sea quilt; color photo, page F1.)

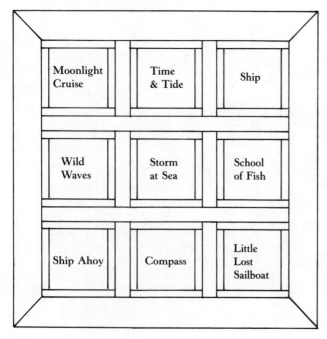

Requirements

	MEASURE-MENTS	NUM-BER	YARDAGE
Finished Size	$41 \times 41''$		
Blocks	8″ square	9	$\frac{1}{2}$ yard each of 5 fabrics
Block Borders	$\frac{3}{4}''$ wide		$\frac{1}{2}$ yard
Horizontal	$1\frac{1}{4} \times 10''$	18	
Vertical	$1\frac{1}{4} \times 8\frac{1}{2}''$	18	
Stripping	2″ wide		$\frac{3}{8}$ yard
Horizontal	$2\frac{1}{2} \times 33''$	2	
Vertical	$2\frac{1}{2} \times 9\frac{1}{2}''$	6	
Border	4″ wide		$\frac{5}{8}$ yard
	$4\frac{1}{2} \times 41\frac{1}{2}''$	4	
Back	$41\frac{1}{2} \times 41\frac{1}{2}''$	1	$1\frac{1}{4}$ yards
Binding	$2 \times 168''$	1	$\frac{1}{2}$ yard

9-Block Quilt

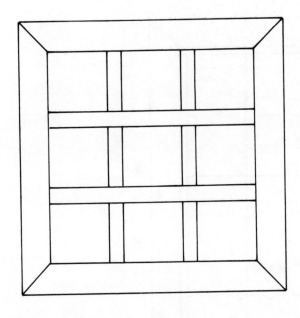

Requirements

	MEASURE-MENTS	NUM-BER	YARDAGE
Finished Size	36 × 36″		
Blocks	8″ square	9	$\frac{1}{2}$ yard each of 5 fabrics
Stripping Horizontal Vertical	2″ wide $2\frac{1}{2} \times 28\frac{1}{2}″$ $2\frac{1}{2} \times 8\frac{1}{2}″$	 2 6	$\frac{1}{4}$ yard
Border Vertical	4″ wide $4\frac{1}{2} \times 36\frac{1}{2}″$	 4	$\frac{5}{8}$ yard
Back	37 × 37″	1	$1\frac{1}{8}$ yards
Binding	2 × 148″	1	$\frac{1}{2}$ yard

12-Block Quilt

(Style of Toys & Games quilt; color photo, page A1.)

Snail Hop	Jack-in-the-Box	Charades
Go In-and-Out the Window	Follow the Leader	Monkey in the Middle
Blind Man's Buff	Cat's Cradle	Simon Says
Farmer in the Dell	Red Light/ Green Light	Kaleido-scope

Requirements

	MEASURE-MENTS	NUM-BER	YARDAGE
Finished Size	36 × 46″		
Blocks	8″ square	12	$\frac{3}{8}$ yard each of 8 fabrics
Stripping Horizontal Vertical	2″ wide $2\frac{1}{2} \times 28\frac{1}{2}″$ $2\frac{1}{2} \times 8\frac{1}{2}″$	 3 8	$\frac{3}{8}$ yard
Border Horizontal Vertical	4″ wide $4\frac{1}{2} \times 36\frac{1}{2}″$ $4\frac{1}{2} \times 46\frac{1}{2}″$	 2 2	$1\frac{3}{8}$ yard2
Back	37 × 47″	1	$1\frac{3}{8}$ yard2
Binding	2 × 168″	1	$\frac{1}{2}$ yard

Note: Buy only $1\frac{3}{8}$ yards if you are making the stripping and border from the same fabric.

15-Block Quilt

(Style of Flowers quilt; color photo, page D1.)

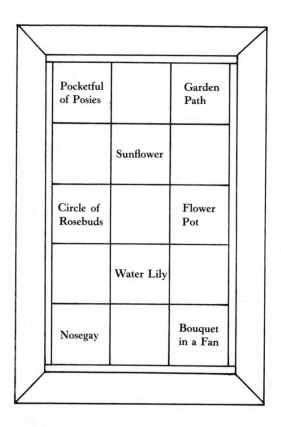

Requirements

	MEASUREMENTS	NUMBER	YARDAGE
Finished Size	34 × 50″		
Blocks	8″ square	15	
Pieced		8	$\frac{3}{8}$ yard each of 6 fabrics
Plain		7	$\frac{1}{2}$ yard
Stripping	none		
Inner Border	1″ wide		$\frac{1}{4}$ yard
Horizontal	$1\frac{1}{2} \times 26\frac{1}{2}$″	2	
Vertical	$1\frac{1}{2} \times 40\frac{1}{2}$″	2	
Outer Border	4″ wide		$1\frac{1}{2}$ yards
Horizontal	$4\frac{1}{2} \times 34\frac{1}{2}$″	2	
Vertical	$4\frac{1}{2} \times 50\frac{1}{2}$″	2	
Back	35 × 51″	1	$1\frac{1}{2}$ yards
Binding	2 × 172″	1	$\frac{1}{2}$ yard

Note: Buy only $1\frac{1}{2}$ yards if you are making the plain blocks and the outer border from the same fabric.

Fancy 15-Block Quilt

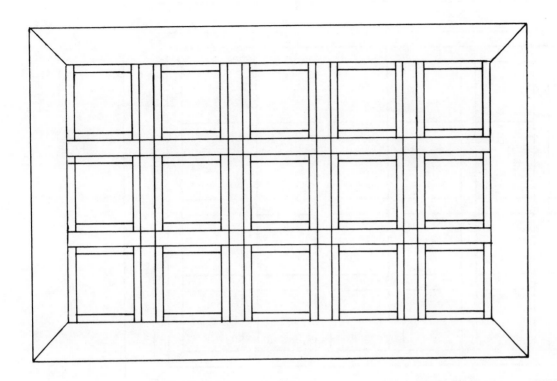

Requirements

	MEASUREMENTS	NUMBER	YARDAGE
Finished Size	$44 \times 68''$		
Blocks	$8''$ square	15	$\frac{1}{2}$ yard each of 6 fabrics
Block Borders Horizontal Vertical	$1''$ wide $1\frac{1}{2} \times 10\frac{1}{2}''$ $1\frac{1}{2} \times 8\frac{1}{2}''$	30 30	$\frac{5}{8}$ yard
Stripping Strips Squares	$2''$ wide $2\frac{1}{2} \times 10\frac{1}{2}''$ $2\frac{1}{2} \times 2\frac{1}{2}''$	22 8	$\frac{1}{2}$ yard $\frac{1}{8}$ yard
Border Horizontal Vertical	$5''$ wide $5\frac{1}{2} \times 44\frac{1}{2}''$ $5\frac{1}{2} \times 68\frac{1}{2}''$	2 2	$1\frac{3}{4}$ yards
Back	$23 \times 69''$	2	4 yards
Binding	$2 \times 228''$	1	$\frac{1}{2}$ yard

Note: For a pretty effect, make the borders and strippings from the same fabric; make the blocks (in the stripping) from a contrasting fabric. If you decide to make your quilt this way, buy only $1\frac{3}{4}$ yards for the borders and stripping.

24-Block Quilt

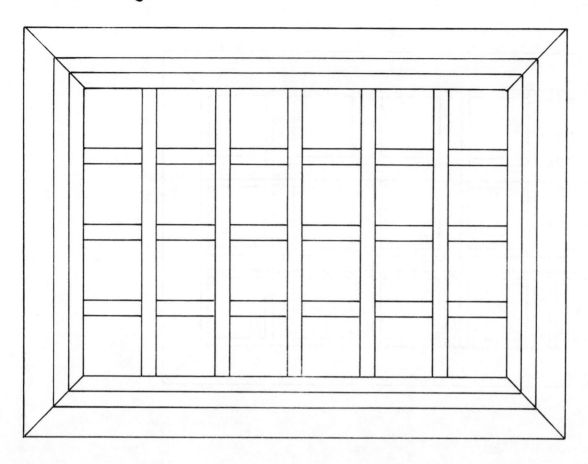

Requirements

	MEASUREMENTS	NUMBER	YARDAGE
Finished Size	$54 \times 74''$		
Blocks	$8''$ square	24	$1\frac{1}{2}$ yards each of 6 fabrics
Stripping Horizontal Vertical	$2''$ wide $2\frac{1}{2} \times 38\frac{1}{2}''$ $2\frac{1}{2} \times 8\frac{1}{2}''$	5 18	$\frac{1}{2}$ yard
Inner Border Horizontal Vertical	$2''$ wide $2\frac{1}{2} \times 42\frac{1}{2}''$ $2\frac{1}{2} \times 62\frac{1}{2}''$	2 2	$1\frac{1}{2}$ yards
Middle Border Horizontal Vertical	$2''$ wide $2\frac{1}{2} \times 46\frac{1}{2}''$ $2\frac{1}{2} \times 66\frac{1}{2}''$	2 2	$1\frac{5}{8}$ yards
Outer Border Horizontal Vertical	$4''$ wide $4\frac{1}{2} \times 54\frac{1}{2}''$ $4\frac{1}{2} \times 74\frac{1}{2}''$	2 2	$1\frac{7}{8}$ yards
Back	$28 \times 75''$	2	$4\frac{1}{8}$ yards
Binding	$2 \times 260''$	1	$\frac{1}{2}$ yard

Note: Buy only $1\frac{7}{8}$ yards if you are making the inner and outer borders from the same fabric. You can avoid buying extra fabric by making the back and the middle border from the same fabric; if you decide to do this, buy only $4\frac{1}{8}$ yards.

DESIGNS

1 **Toys & Games** *Suitable for a boy or girl, the bright crayon colors used in this quilt will bring a smile to your favorite child's face. The pieced binding echoes the fabrics used in the block designs—a visually exciting finishing touch. See page 27 for names of the quilt block designs and the Requirements. (Pieced and quilted by the author.)*

1 **Bright Hopes** The unusual combination of subtle colors make this quilt entirely appropriate for a newborn boy or girl—and an excellent gift for expectant parents. These photos show blends of two pleasant color schemes. Made of only six patchwork blocks, this comforting quilt can be finished quickly, allowing plenty of time for some elaborate quilting. See page 25 for names of the quilt block designs and the Requirements. (Pieced and quilted by the author.)

2 *Grandmother's Favorite (page 169)*

1 *Mother's Dream (page 181)*

2 *Godmother's Gift (page 164)*

C

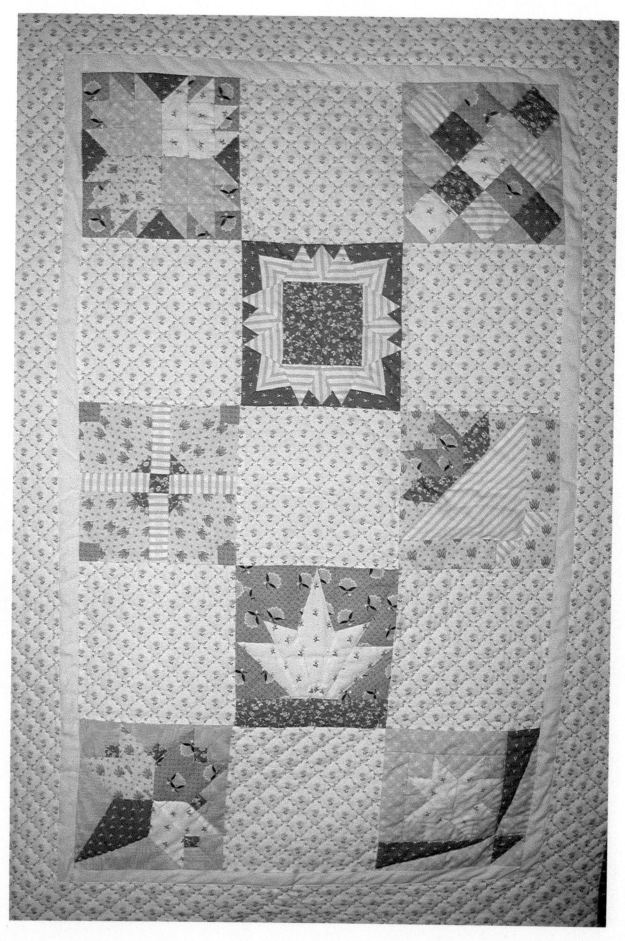

D

1   Pocketful of Posies (page 81)

2   Water Lily (page 92)

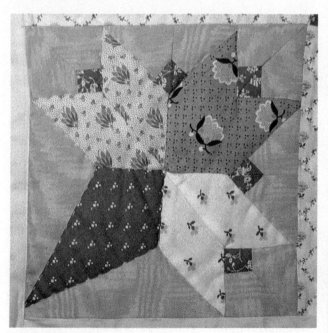

3   Nosegay (page 108)

4   Bouquet in a Fan (page 97)

(Facing page)

1   **Flowers**   This pretty quilt will enchant any little girl, mother and grandmother. Find
a fabric with a delicate trellis motif for the background blocks and border, then coordinate
your other fabrics to it. The quilting is easy—just follow the pattern on the fabric. See
page 28 for names of the quilt block designs and the Requirements. (Pieced by the author
and quilted by Evelyn Macho.)

1 **By the Sea** *You'll have no trouble convincing your little sailor to go to sleep beneath this quilt! Visions of sailboats, oceans and flying fish will happily lull him or her to dreamland. This quilt also makes a spectacular wall hanging. See page 26 for names of the quilt block designs and the Requirements. (Pieced and quilted by Jean Kubitz.)*

1   Moonlight Cruise (page 34)

2   Ship (page 43)

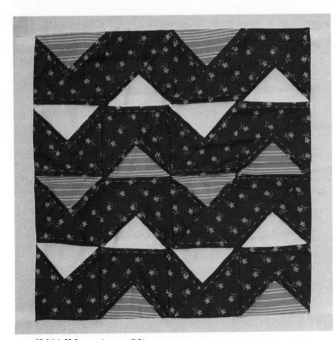

3   Wild Waves (page 33)

4   Compass (page 37)

1   *Follow the Leader (page 141)*

2   *Cat's Cradle (page 138)*

3   *Red Light/Green Light (page 147)*

4   *Kaleidoscope (page 148)*

H

By the Sea

Wild Waves

(Color photos, pages F1 and G3)

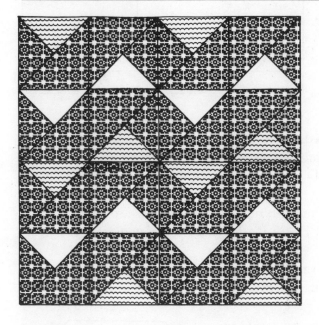

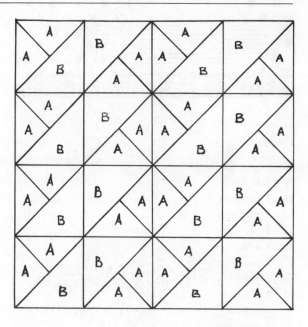

Composed of 16 pieced squares, this block may take more time to complete, but the sewing is all straight and easy.

Following the diagram, construct all the A triangles by sewing a dark A to a white or bright A. Sew each of the pieced triangles to a B to complete each square. Arrange the squares as shown in the diagram. Sew the squares together in horizontal rows; then sew the rows together, matching seams carefully to complete the design.

Outline-quilt each white and bright triangle; quilt the remainder of the block in a wave pattern.

EASY

Pieces per block: 48
A   8 white, 8 bright, 16 dark
B   16 dark

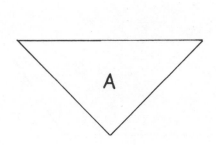

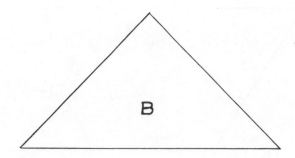

33

Moonlight Cruise

(Color photos, pages F1 and G1)

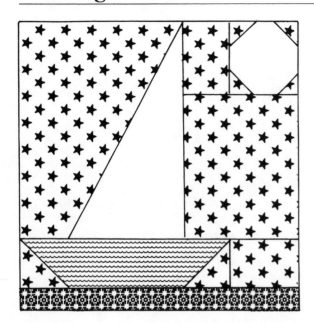
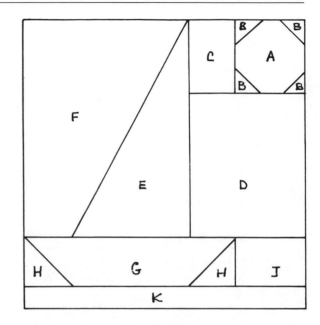

EASY

Pieces per block: 14

A   1 light
B   4 medium
C   1 medium
D   1 medium
E   1 white
F   1 medium
G   1 bright
H   1 medium + 1 medium
     reversed
J   1 medium
K   1 dark

Sew a B to each short edge of A to complete the moon square. Sew C to a side of the moon square. Sew D below C and the moon square as shown in the diagram. Sew C-D to E, then sew E to F to complete the upper portion of the block.

For the hull portion of the sailboat, sew an H to each side of G, then sew J to H. Sew K to H-G-H-J. Sew the top and bottom portions together to complete the design.

Outline-quilt the sailboat and moon. Quilt a wave pattern on the K piece; quilt a swirling cloud pattern across the sky.

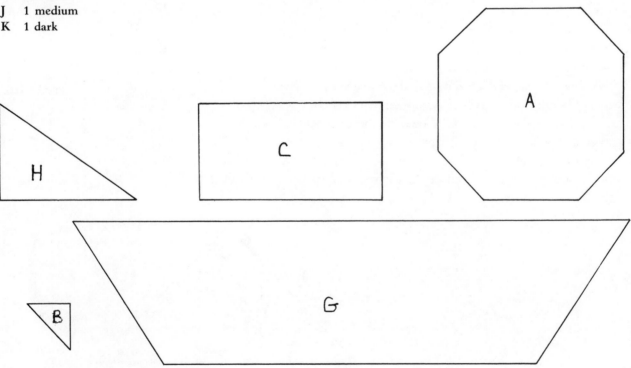

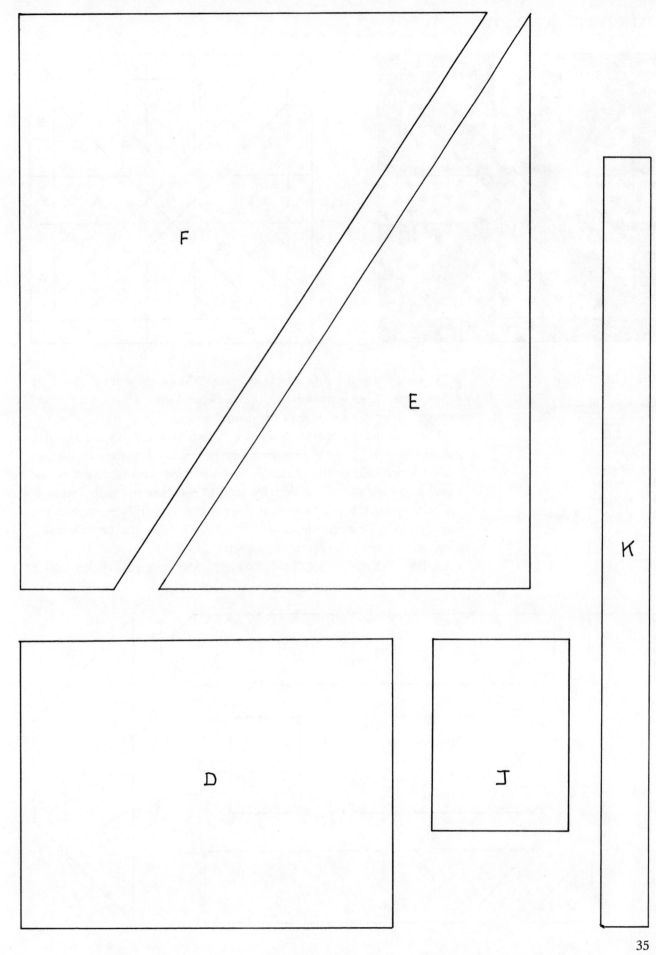

Anchors Aweigh

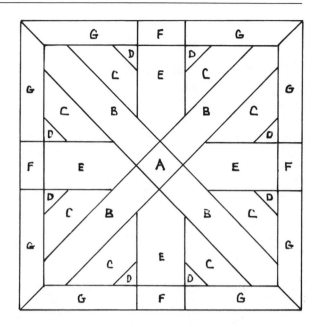

CHALLENGING

Pieces per block: 37

A 1 bright
B 4 dark
C 8 bright
D 8 dark
E 4 bright
F 4 bright
G 4 dark + 4 dark reversed

Construct this dramatic block in 2 steps. Make the central square by sewing a triangle to each side of the diagonal strip. Then assemble and sew the border to each edge of the central square.

For the central diagonal strip, sew a B to each side of A. For the triangles, sew a D to each C; sew C-D to each side of E. Then sew the triangles just made to each side of the remaining B's, following the diagram. Sew the triangles to each side of the diagonal strip to complete the central square.

For the border, sew a G to each short side of each F, being sure to use reversed pieces for each strip. Sew G-F-G to each side of the central square. Mitre the corners to complete the design.

Outline-quilt the anchors; quilt a wave pattern across the background.

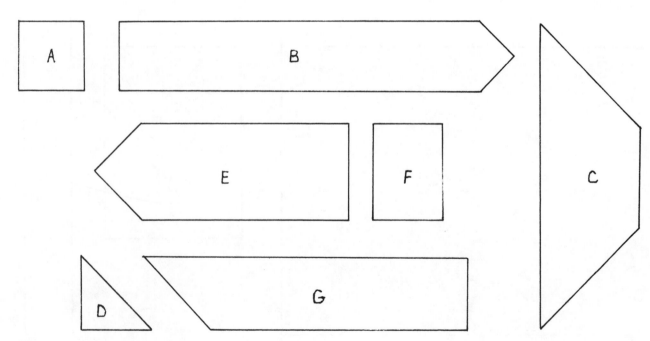

Compass

(Color photos, pages F1 and G4)

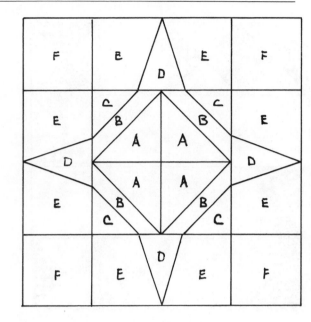

The middle of this block has 4 pieced squares; the border has 4 pieced rectangles and 4 squares.

Construct the central squares first. Join A to B, then sew C to B, completing each square. Sew the squares together forming the halves as shown in the diagram. Then sew the halves together to complete the central square.

Sew an E to each side of a D, forming 4 rectangles; be sure to use reversed pieces for each. Sew a rectangle to each side of the central square. Sew an F to each side of the remaining rectangles for the top and bottom strips. Sew the top and bottom strips to the middle to complete the design.

Quilt the block to emphasize the compass; quilt a wave pattern across the background.

EASY

Pieces per block: 28
A 2 white, 2 dark
B 4 bright
C 4 medium
D 4 bright
E 4 medium + 4 medium reversed
F 4 medium

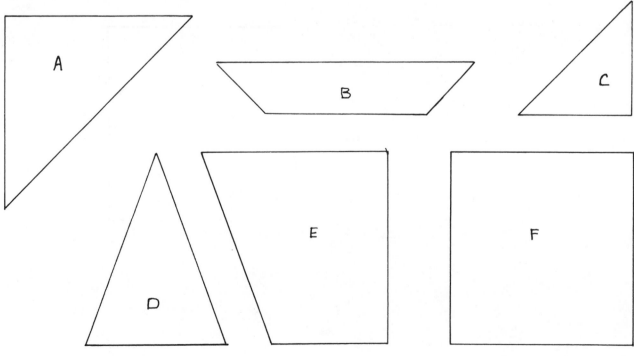

Flying Fish

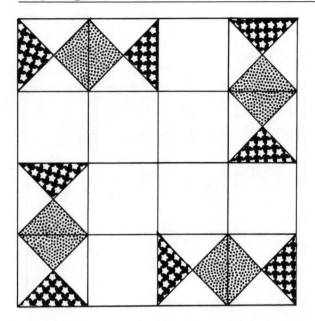

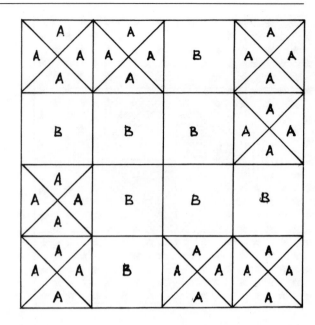

EASY

Pieces per block: 40
A 16 light, 8 medium, 8 dark
B 8 light

You can create interesting color combinations in this block. Use your scraps to make the wings and bodies in a rainbow of different fabrics.

Assemble the A squares first. Sew a light A to a medium or dark A, creating each half of each square. Sew the halves together to complete the squares, making sure you have a medium and dark A in each.

Position the squares as shown in the diagram, then assemble in 4 rows. Sew the rows together, matching seams carefully, to complete the design.

Outline-quilt each of the flying fish. Quilt a cloud pattern across the background pieces.

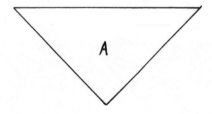

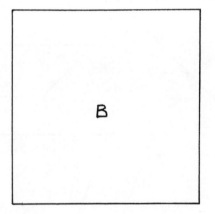

Life Preserver

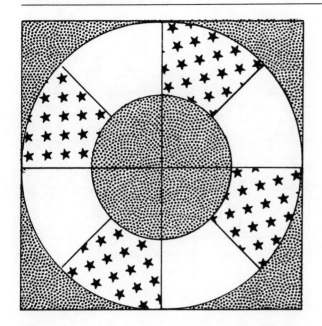

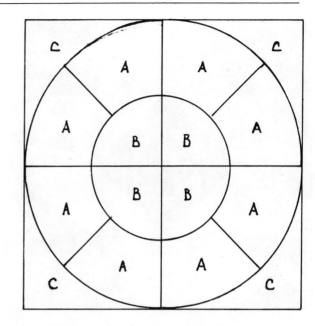

E ach of the 4 pieced squares in this block has 2 curved seams, making the assembly a bit difficult. See Sewing Curves (page 16).

Sew each light A to a medium A first. Sew a B to each concave edge of A-A; sew a C to each convex edge. Sew together 2 of the pieced squares to form each half of the block. Sew the halves together to complete the design.

Quilt the block in concentric circles.

CHALLENGING

Pieces per block: 16
A 4 light, 4 medium
B 4 dark
C 4 dark

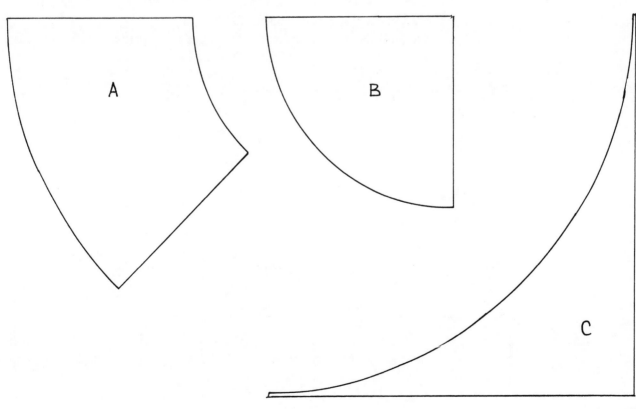

Rough Seas

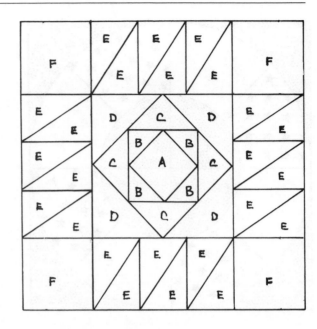

CHALLENGING

Pieces per block: 41

A 1 dark
B 4 medium
C 4 dark
D 4 medium
E 8 light, 12 medium
 reversed, 4 dark
F 4 dark

Although this striking block takes some time to assemble, it makes an excellent central block in any sampler quilt.

Assemble the central square first, then add the border to the edges. To assemble the square, sew a B to each edge of A. Sew a C to each B-B edge. Sew a D to each C-C edge.

For the border, sew a medium E to each light and dark E. Arrange the E and F pieces around the central square as shown in the diagram. Sew the E-E pieces together. Sew 2 of the strips just made to each side of the middle. Sew an F to each end of the remaining E strips, then sew to the top and bottom of the block to complete the design.

Outline-quilt the medium pieces; quilt a wave pattern across the dark pieces.

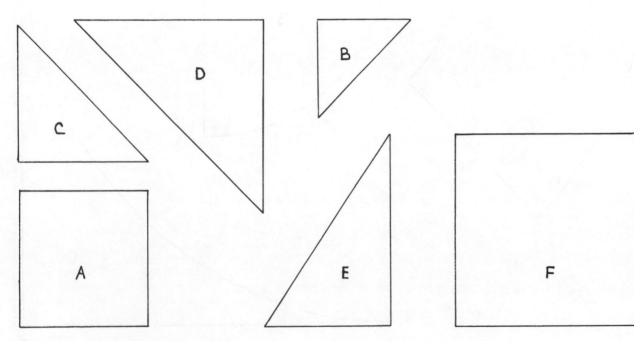

Sailboats

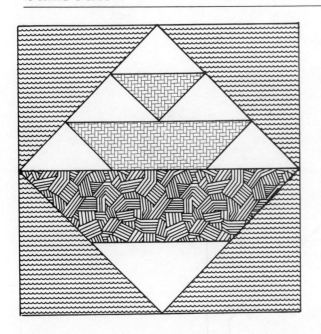

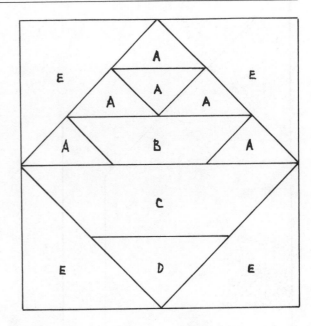

A central square bordered by 4 triangles makes this design quite easy to sew.

Make the central square first. Assemble the A's to complete the top triangle as shown in the diagram. Sew a light A to each short side of B; sew to the top triangle. Sew C to A-B-A. Sew D to C. Sew an E to each edge of the central square to complete the design.

Outline-quilt the light pieces; crosshatch C and medium A and B. Quilt a wave pattern across the E pieces.

EASY

Pieces per block: 13
A 5 light, 1 medium
B 1 medium
C 1 dark
D 1 light
E 4 bright

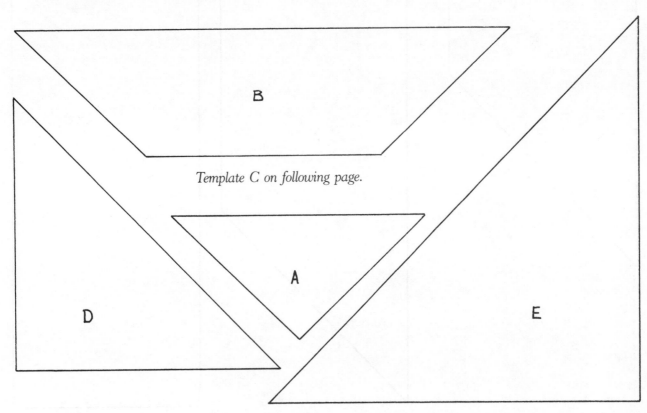

Template C on following page.

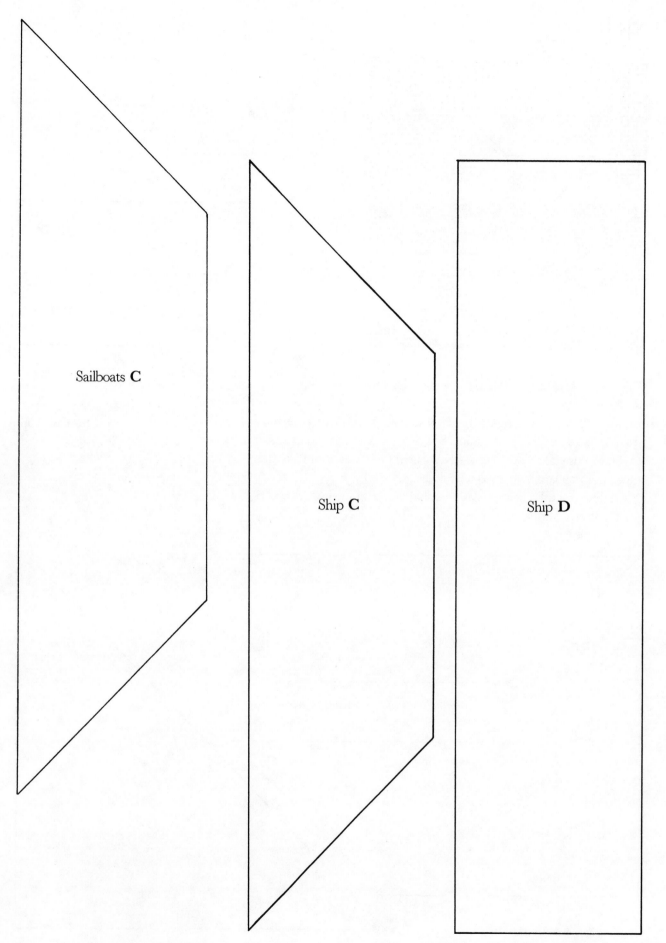

Sailboats **C**

Ship **C**

Ship **D**

Ship

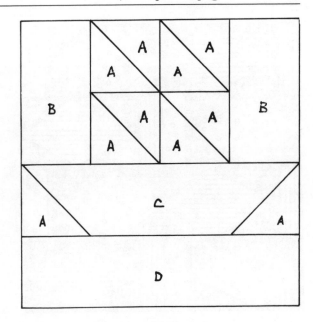

Construct the sails square first by sewing each light A to a dark A, forming 4 squares. Sew 2 squares together to form each half of the sails square as shown in the diagram. Then sew the halves together to complete the square.

Sew a B to each side of the sails square to complete the top half of the block. To construct the bottom half, sew an A to each angled edge of C. Then sew D to A-C-A. Sew the top and bottom halves together to complete the design.

Outline-quilt the white sails and the hull of the ship. Quilt a wave pattern across the D piece.

EASY

Pieces per block: 14
A 4 white, 6 dark
B 2 dark
C 1 bright
D 1 light

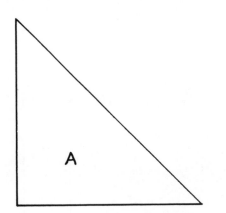

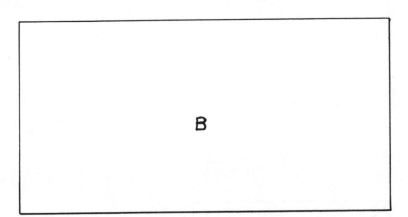

Templates C and D on facing page.

School of Fish

(Color photo, page F1)

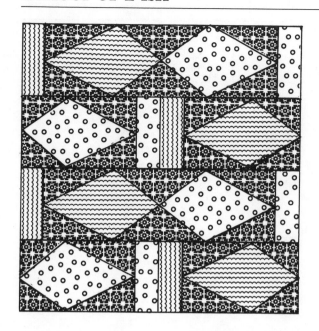

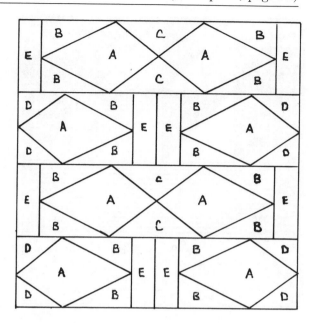

MODERATE

Pieces per block: 44

A   4 light, 4 bright
B   8 dark + 8 dark reversed
C   4 dark
D   4 dark + 4 dark reversed
E   4 light, 4 bright

For a striking effect, make each fish in a different fabric in this block, which is constructed in 4 horizontal strips.

Begin by constructing the first and third strips. Sew a B to each long edge of A. Sew an E to each B end. Sew a C to each of the halves of the strip along opposite A edges. Sew the halves of the strip together along the A-C edges.

Next, construct the second and fourth strips. Sew a B to each long edge of A. Sew an E to each B end. Sew a D to each short edge of A. Sew the halves of the strip together along the E edges. Sew the 4 strips together alternately to complete the design.

Outline-quilt each fish. Quilt a wave pattern on the background pieces.

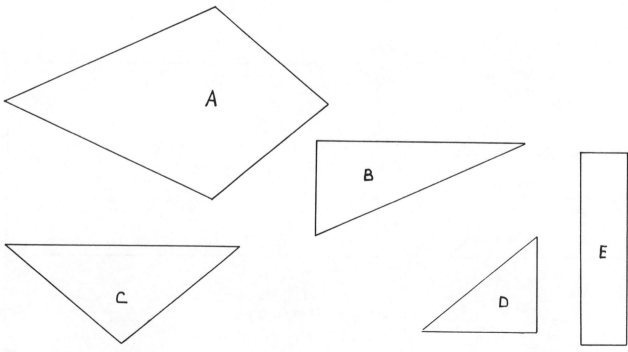

Ship Ahoy

(Color photo, page F1)

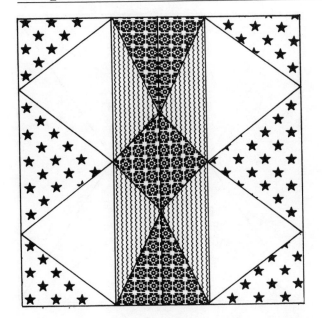

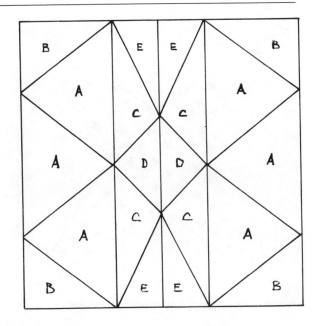

Construct this block in 4 horizontal strips: 2 outer sail strips and 2 inner hull strips.

Assemble the sail strips first. Sew a white A to each side of a medium A. Sew a B to each white A to complete each strip. Next, construct the hull strips by sewing a C to each side of a D. Sew an E to each C to complete each strip. Sew the sail strips to the hull strips. Then, matching seams carefully, sew the hull strips together to complete the design.

Outline-quilt each sail and hull. Quilt a wave pattern on the D and E pieces.

MODERATE

Pieces per block: 20
A 4 white, 2 medium
B 2 medium + 2 medium reversed
C 2 bright + 2 bright reversed
D 2 dark
E 2 dark + 2 dark reversed

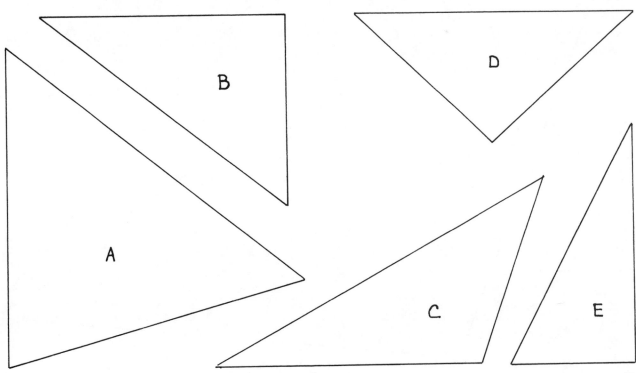

Starfish

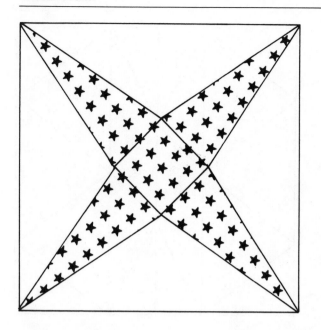
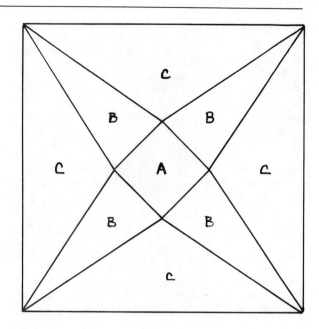

CHALLENGING

Pieces per block: 9
A   1 bright
B   4 bright
C   4 light

Although this block is composed of only 9 pieces, it is challenging because each C piece must be inset into the starfish; see How to Inset (page 15).

Sew a B to each edge of A. Inset a C into each of the angles to complete the design.

Outline-quilt the starfish; quilt a wave pattern across the C pieces.

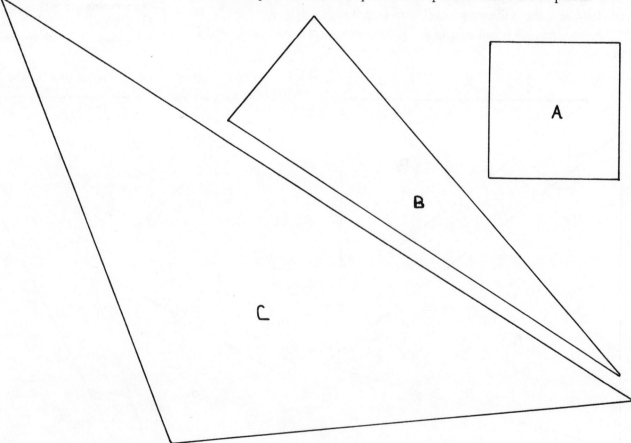

Star of the Sea

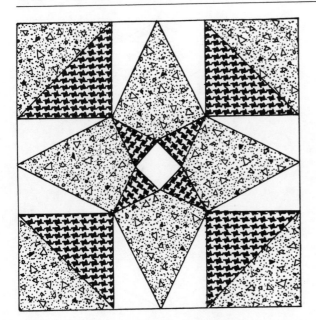

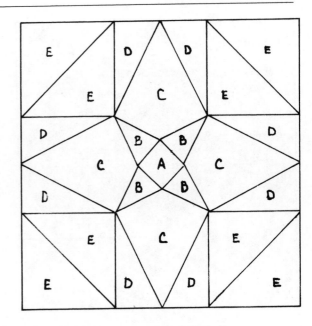

Does this design appear easy? It isn't. There are 2 separate sections where pieces are inset into one another; see How to Inset (page 15). Accurate marking and cutting are essential.

Sew a B to each edge of A first. Sew a D to each long edge of C. Inset the short edges of each C into the angles made by the B pieces. Sew each medium E to a dark E. Inset each E square into the angles made by the D pieces to complete the design.

Quilt around the B, C and dark E pieces.

CHALLENGING

Pieces per block: 25

A	1 light
B	4 dark
C	4 medium
D	4 light + 4 light reversed
E	4 medium, 4 dark

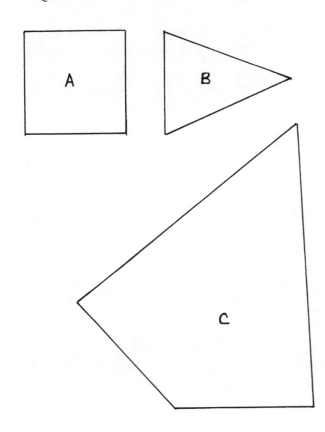

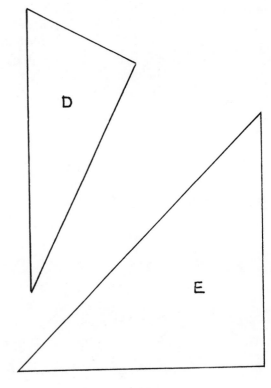

Storm at Sea

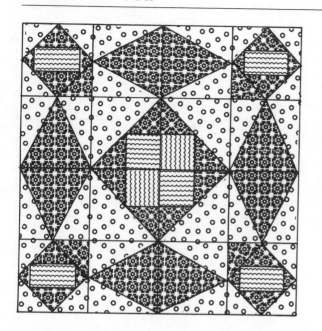

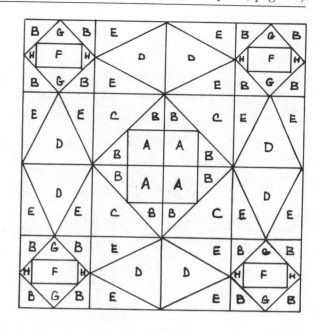

CHALLENGING

Pieces per block: 76

A	4 bright
B	12 light, 12 dark
C	4 light
D	8 dark
E	8 light + 8 light reversed
F	4 bright
G	8 dark
H	8 dark

The challenge of this block is to assemble the pieces to accentuate all the points of the triangles and squares. Accurate cutting and piecing are essential. Study the block and observe that it is composed of 16 pieced squares.

Begin with the central squares. Sew a dark B to adjacent sides of A. Sew a C to the long edge of the triangle you just made. Next, construct the border squares by sewing an E to the long edges of each D. Finally, construct the corner squares. Sew a G to the long edges of each F; then sew an H to each short edge of the F. Sew a B to each G-H edge to complete the square.

Arrange the 16 pieced squares following the diagram. Assemble the squares in horizontal rows, then join the rows, matching seams carefully, to complete the design.

Quilt the block to emphasize the dark pieces, which give a curved effect to the design.

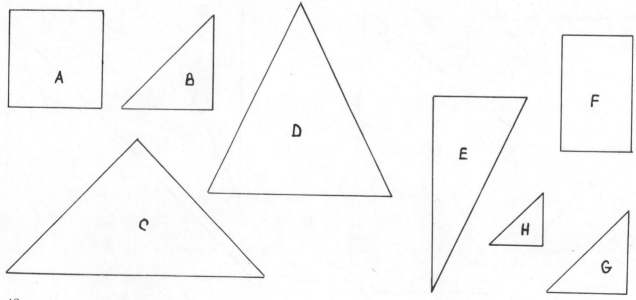

Time & Tide

(Color photo, page F1)

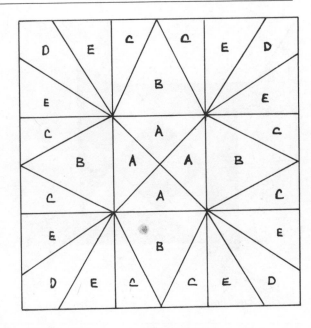

Composed of 9 pieced squares, this design requires accuracy in cutting and piecing to achieve the perfect points of the D pieces.

Begin with the central square; sew 2 A's together to form each half of the middle. Sew the halves together to form the square. Next, construct the 4 squares adjacent to the middle by sewing a C to each side of a B, following the diagram for color placement. Next, construct the corner squares by sewing an E to the sides of each D. Arrange the squares following the diagram; sew together in horizontal rows. Sew the rows together, matching seams carefully, to complete the design.

Quilt around the central star and the four D pieces.

MODERATE

Pieces per block: 28

A   4 bright

B   2 medium, 2 dark

C   2 medium + 2 medium reversed, 2 dark + 2 dark reversed

D   4 bright

E   2 medium + 2 medium reversed
    2 dark + 2 dark reversed

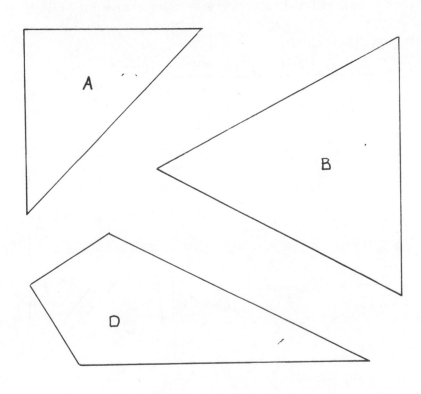

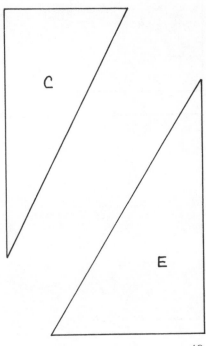

Whirlpool

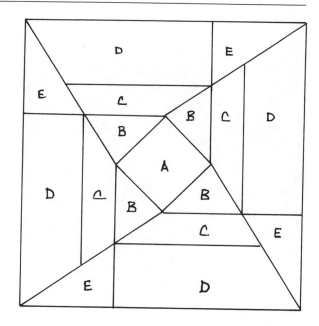

CHALLENGING

Pieces per block: 17

A 1 dark
B 4 light
C 4 dark
D 4 light
E 4 medium

Precision and accuracy are needed to match all the seams and corners. This challenging block is quite attractive when created in 3 shades of blue.

To begin, sew a B to each edge of A as shown in the diagram. Sew a C to each B, turning your stitching sharply at the corner of A to sew the short edge of C to the adjacent B piece. Sew an E to each straight side edge of D. Sew the first D to C. Sew subsequent D-E pieces in a clockwise direction around the middle, turning your stitching to join E to the adjacent C-D pieces. Connect the first E to the last C-D to complete the design.

An alternate and easier method of assembly is to sew B to C, C to D and D to E. Sew C-D-E to B-C-D in a clockwise manner, leaving the middle unsewn. Appliqué A over the middle to complete the design; see How to Appliqué (page 16).

Quilt the block in concentric circles to simulate a whirlpool.

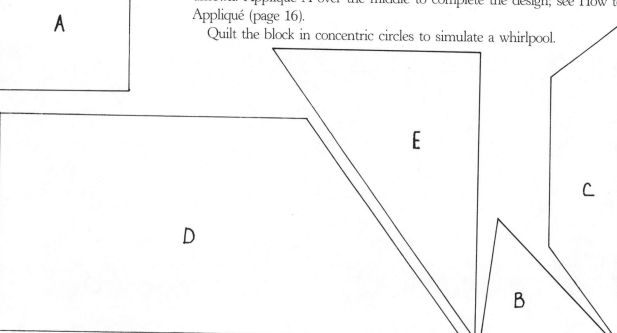

Ocean Waves

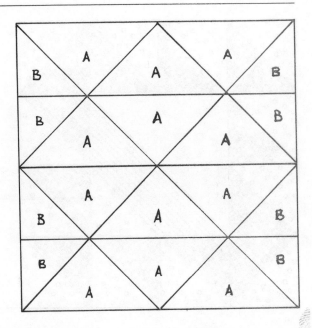

If made in blue and white, this dramatic block looks like moving waves. It is easily assembled in 4 horizontal rows.

To make each row, sew the dark and light A's together, following the diagram. Sew a B to the end of each row. Sew the rows together, matching points of triangles carefully, to complete the design.

Quilt a wave pattern across the block, ignoring the seams.

EASY

Pieces per block: 20
A   6 light, 6 dark
B   4 light, 4 dark

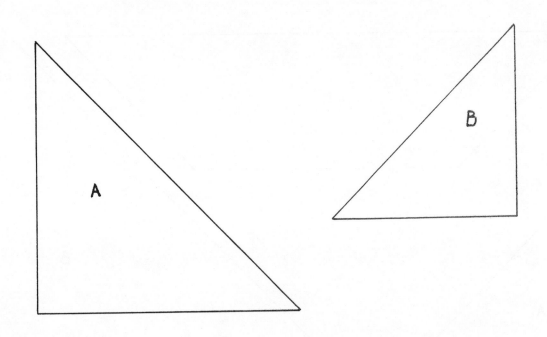

Little Lost Sailboat

(Color photo, page F1)

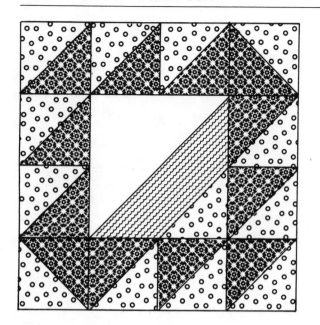

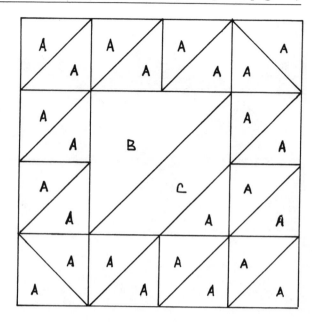

EASY

Pieces per block: 27
A   13 light, 12 dark
B   1 white
C   1 bright

Construct the sailboat first by sewing a light A to C, and then B to C. Next, construct all the A squares by sewing the light and dark A's together. Arrange all the pieces as shown in the diagram. Sew the 2 pairs of A squares on each side together; sew to each side of the central section.

Sew 4 A squares together for the top and bottom strips. Sew to the middle to complete the design.

Quilt around the sailboat and each dark A square.

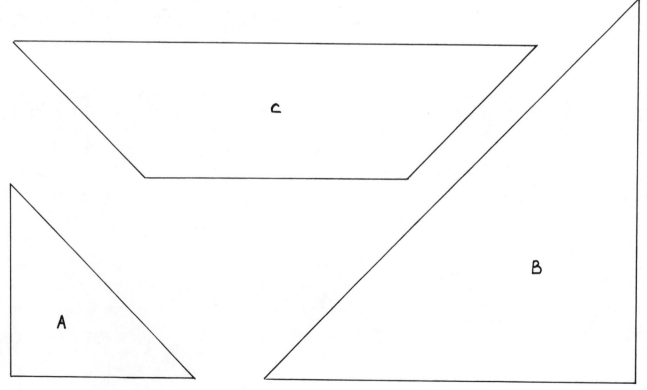

Outdoor Fun

Kites

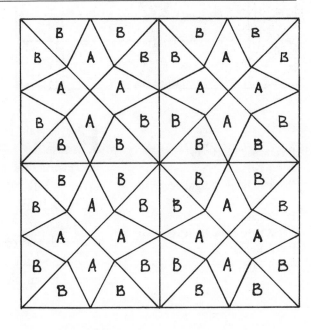

What a vibrant design this is when the kites are made in bright fabrics that contrast sharply with the light and dark background fabrics! The design is composed of 4 squares with 4 triangles in each square.

To make each triangle, sew a B to each side of A, being careful to follow the design for placement of colors. Sew together 2 pairs of A-B triangles to create the halves of each square. Sew the halves together, matching seams carefully, to complete each kite square. Sew 2 pairs of squares together to make each half of the block. Sew the halves together to complete the design.

Quilt around each kite; quilt a cloud pattern across the background.

MODERATE

Pieces per block: 48
A 4 bright I, 4 bright II, 4 medium I, 4 medium II
B 8 light + 8 light reversed, 8 dark + 8 dark reversed

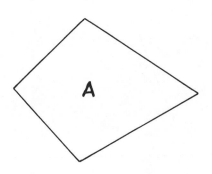

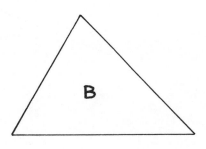

Airplane

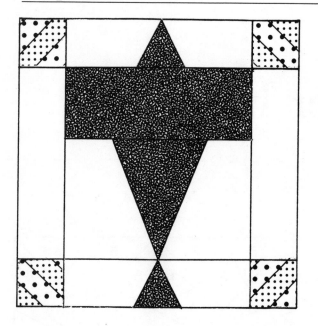

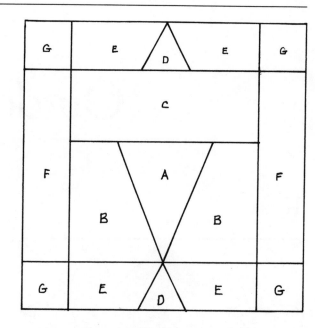

EASY

Pieces per block: 16

A   1 dark
B   1 light + 1 light reversed
C   1 dark
D   2 dark
E   2 light + 2 light reversed
F   2 light
G   4 bright

For anyone interested in flying—and what child isn't?—this design is a must.

Construct the central square first. Sew a B to each side of A. Sew C to the top of B-A-B. Next, assemble the top and bottom borders. Sew an E to each side of D, being sure to use reversed pieces. Sew to the top and bottom of the central square as shown in the diagram. Finally, make the side borders. Sew a G to each end of F. Sew to each side of the middle to complete the design.

Outline-quilt the airplane, then quilt a swirling pattern across the background to simulate clouds.

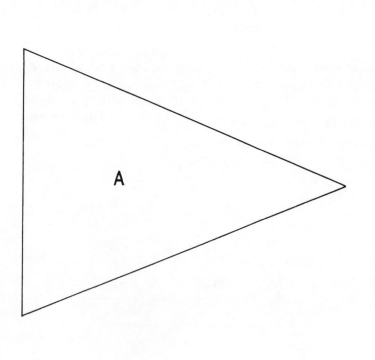

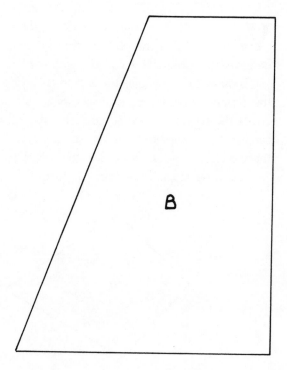

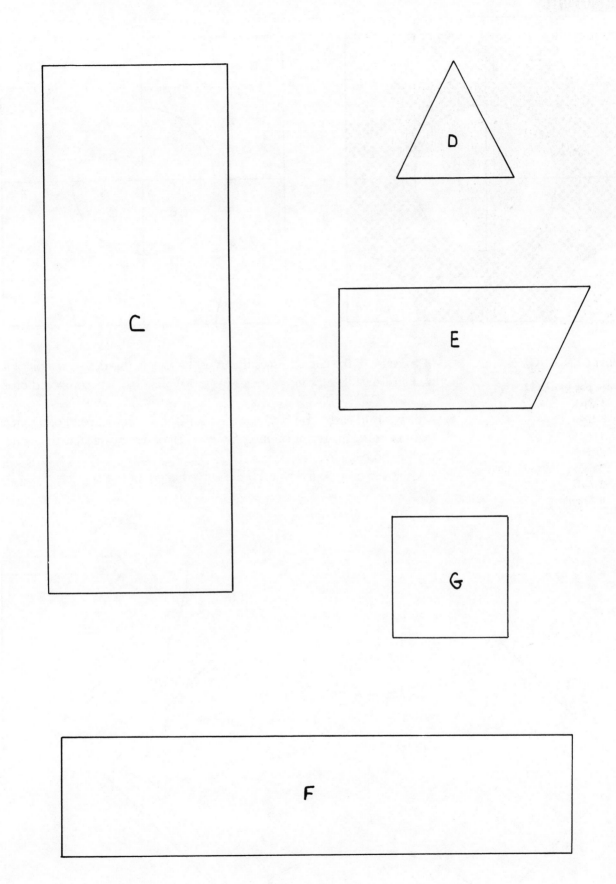

Baseball

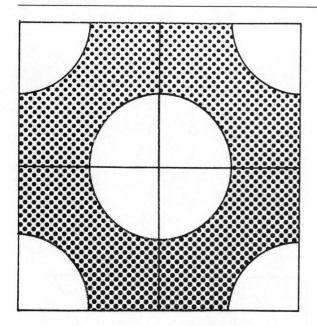 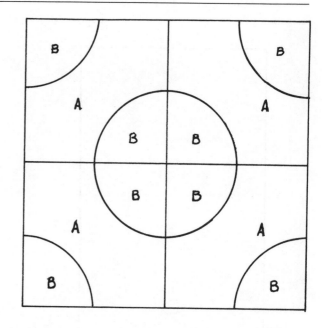

CHALLENGING

Pieces per block: 12
A   4 dark
B   8 light

Because of the curved edges that must be joined, this design is a bit of a challenge. See Sewing Curves (page 16). The block is composed of 4 squares.

Sew a B to each edge of A, easing each B to fit. Sew 2 pairs of squares together, matching seams carefully for each half of the square. Sew the halves together to complete the design.

Quilt the background to echo the curved edges of the B pieces.

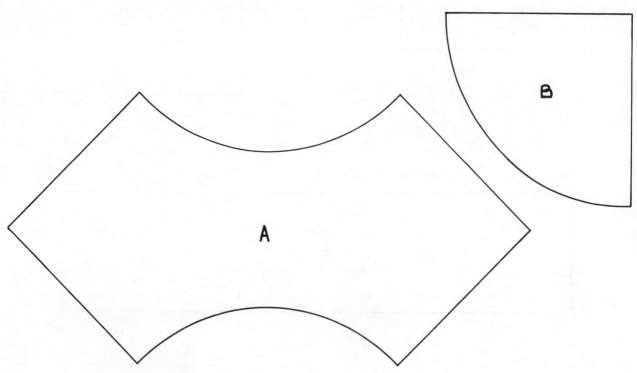

Falling Leaves

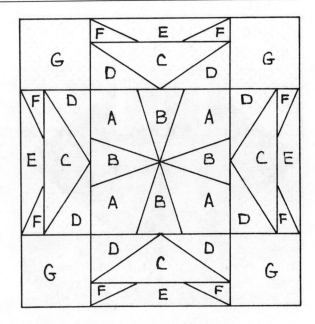

When made up in light and dark fabrics, this design appears almost like an optical illusion. It also looks dramatic when the 4 leaves are made up in various autumnal hues.

Construct the central square first. Sew each A to a B. Sew 2 pairs of A-B pieces together for each half of the square. Then sew the halves together, matching all seams in the middle. For each of the pieced borders, sew a D to each edge of C. Sew an F to each edge of E. Sew D-C-D to F-E-F following the diagram. Sew 2 of the strips just made to each side of the central square. Sew a G to each end of the remaining strips, then sew to the top and bottom of the middle to complete the design.

Quilt the outline of each leaf and then quilt a pattern of veins in the middle of each one.

MODERATE

Pieces per block: 36

A   4 dark
B   4 light
C   4 light
D   4 dark + 4 dark reversed
E   4 light
F   4 dark + 4 dark reversed
G   4 dark

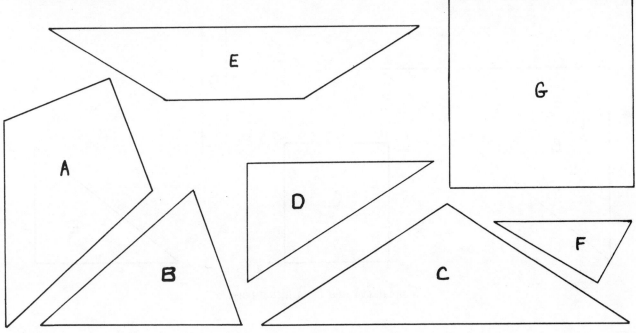

Football

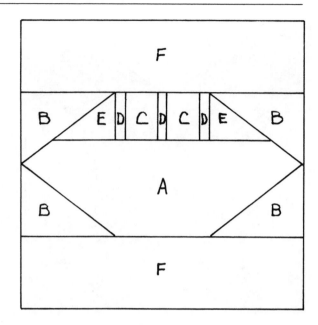

MODERATE

Pieces per block: 14

A   1 dark
B   2 bright + 2 bright
    reversed
C   2 dark
D   3 light
E   1 dark + 1 dark reversed
F   1 bright, 1 medium

Young sports enthusiasts will be thrilled to own a quilt displaying a variety of their favorite games. This football design is a good block to feature in such a quilt.

To make the football, sew a B to opposite sides of A. Assemble the top by alternately sewing the D and C pieces together; sew an E to each end D. Sew a B to each E; then sew the strip to the bottom of the football. Sew a bright F to the top and a medium F to the bottom of the football to complete the design.

Quilt vertical lines across the medium F to simulate grass. Outline-quilt the football and laces, then quilt a swirling cloud pattern across the sky.

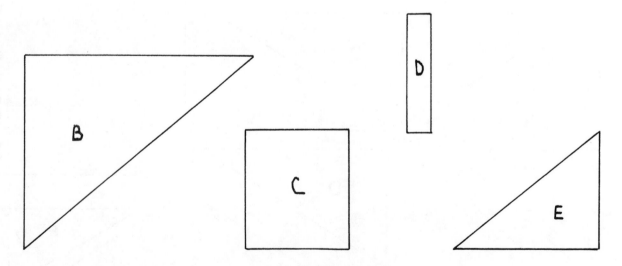

Templates A and F on facing page.

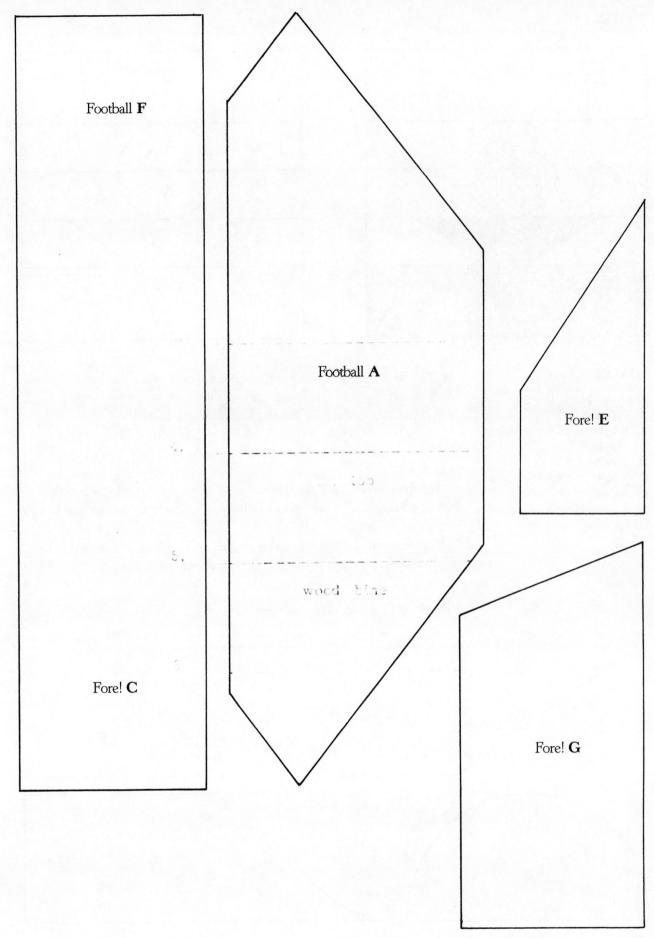

Football **F**

Football **A**

too

wood bine

Fore! **C**

Fore! **E**

Fore! **G**

Fore!

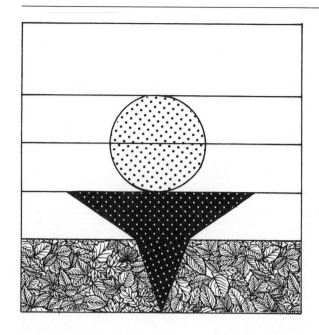

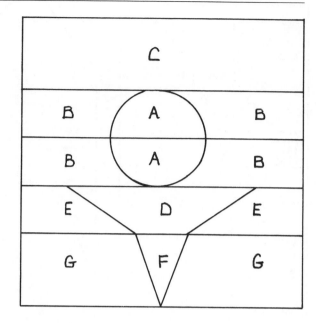

CHALLENGING

Pieces per block: 13

A   2 bright
B   2 light + 2 light reversed
C   1 light
D   1 dark
E   1 light + 1 light reversed
F   1 dark
G   1 medium + 1 medium reversed

No one is more enthusiastic than an avid golfer—and this block will be a favorite for future golf champions! Take your time when sewing the A and B pieces together; see Sewing Curves (page 16).

Sew a B to each side of each A, easing each B to fit the curved edge of A. Sew the B-A-B strips together to complete the golf ball. Sew C to the top edge.

For the tee, sew an E to opposite sides of D. Sew a G to each side of F. Sew E-D-E to G-F-G to complete the tee. Sew the tee to the golf ball to complete the design.

Outline-quilt the golf ball and tee. Quilt vertical lines across the G pieces to simulate grass; quilt a swirling cloud pattern across the sky.

Templates C, E and G on preceding page.

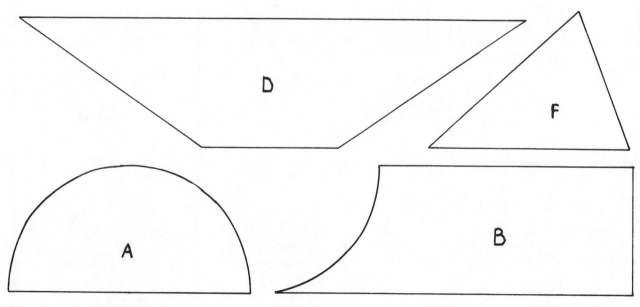

Kite's Tail

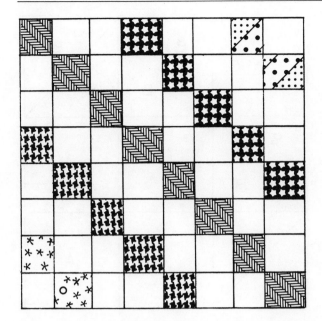

Although the sewing is obviously straight, this block may be tricky to construct because of all the seams that must be matched. Use lots of bright colors to create an exciting block.

Arrange all the squares as shown in the diagram, then sew them together in horizontal rows. Join the rows, matching seams carefully, to complete the design.

Outline-quilt each colored square.

MODERATE

Pieces per block: 64
A 42 light, 2 bright I, 2 bright II, 8 medium, 5 dark I, 5 dark II

Soaring Eagle

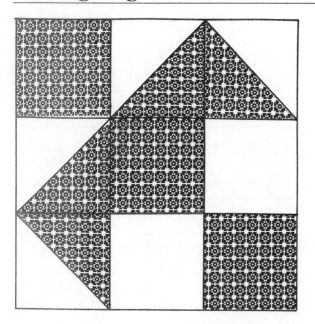

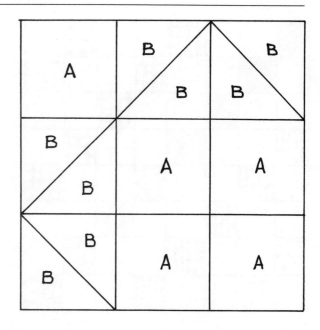

Dramatic and lovely, this design is sure to set children's imaginations soaring! It is easily assembled in 3 rows with 3 blocks in each row.

First, construct all the B squares by sewing each light B to a dark B. Then arrange all the squares as shown in the diagram. Sew together in 3 rows. Join the rows, matching seams carefully, to complete the design.

Quilt a feather pattern across the block.

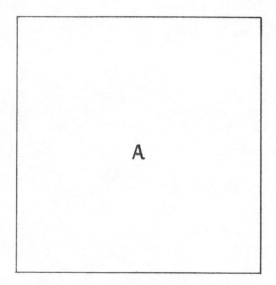

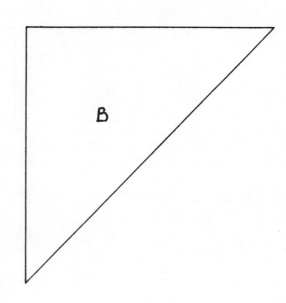

Tail of Benjamin's Kite

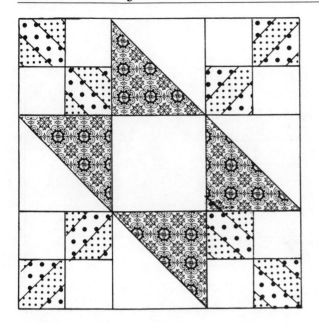

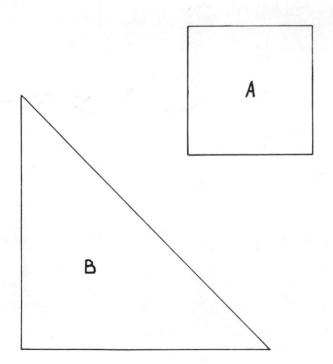

Not only a dynamic design, this block is also easy to construct. Take care to match your seams. Assemble the block in 3 rows with 3 squares in each row.

First, construct the A squares by sewing 4 A's together as shown in the diagram. Next, sew together 4 pairs of light and dark B's to make the B squares. Sew an A square to each side of each B square, following the diagram for the position of the bright A squares. Sew a B square to each side of the C square. Sew the A-B-A strips to each side of the B-C-B strip to complete the design.

Outline-quilt the bright and dark pieces.

MODERATE

Pieces per block: 25
A   8 light, 8 bright
B   4 light, 4 dark
C   1 light

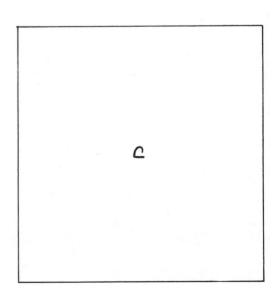

Truck

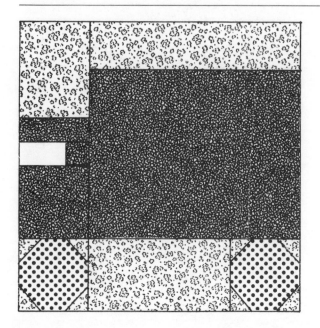

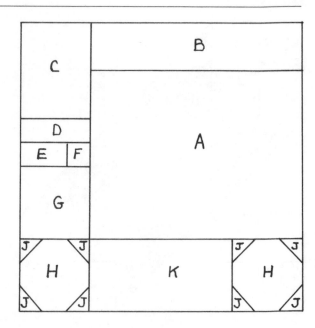

MODERATE

Pieces per block: 18

A	1	dark
B	1	medium
C	1	medium
D	1	dark
E	1	light
F	1	dark
G	1	dark
H	2	bright
J	8	medium
K	1	medium

Trucks hold a mysterious fascination for many boys and girls. Add this design to a gift quilt for a rewarding reaction from your favorite child.

To assemble the truck, sew A to B. Sew C to D. Sew E to F. Then sew E-F to D. Sew G to E-F, then sew the strip just made to A-B.

For the wheels strip, sew a J to each short edge of each H. Sew a wheel to each side of K. Sew the wheels strip to the truck to complete the design.

Outline-quilt the body, cab and wheels of the truck. Quilt a logo or the child's name across the body of the truck. Quilt a cloud pattern across the sky.

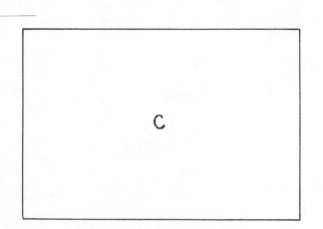

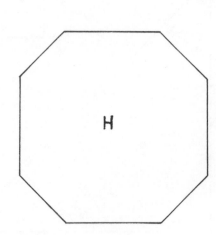

A

B

E

F

J

K

G

Young Man's Fancy

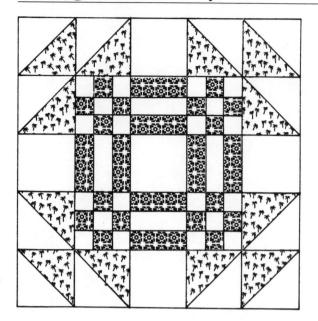

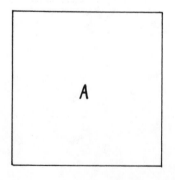

CHALLENGING

Pieces per block: 77

A	5 light
B	4 light, 8 dark
C	20 light, 16 dark
D	12 light, 12 medium

This handsome block requires considerable time to assemble, but your efforts will be rewarded by a beautiful square to enhance your sampler quilt. Construct the central square first, then add the borders.

For the central square, piece all the small B and C squares first. Make the B squares by sewing a dark B to each long edge of a light B. The C squares are made of 9 squares: first, sew together 3 rows of C squares, alternating the colors as shown in the diagram. Then sew the rows together to complete each square. Sew a B square to each side of A. Sew a C square to each side of the remaining B's. Sew C-B-C to each side of B-A-B to complete the central square.

Arrange the remaining A and the D pieces around the central square. Construct all the D squares by sewing the light and medium D's together. Sew a D square to each side of each A. Sew 2 of the strips just made to each side of the central square. Sew the remaining D's to each end of the D-A-D strips, then sew to the top and bottom edges of the block to complete the design.

Outline-quilt all the medium and dark pieces.

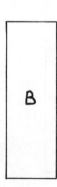

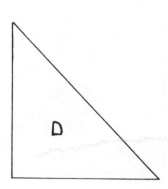

Snips & Snails
& Puppy Dog Tails

Cobweb

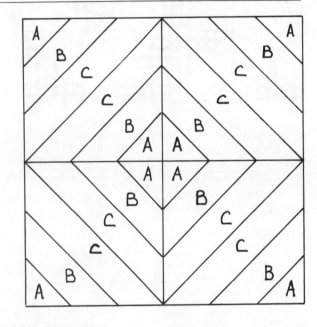

Easily constructed in 4 squares, this design lends itself well to repetition. To create a dramatic crib quilt, make 4 identical Cobweb squares and sew them together without stripping. Subsidiary designs within the quilt will be produced by the outer dark and medium fabrics.

Make each of the 4 squares following the diagram for placement of fabric shades. Sew A to B, B to C, C to C, C to B and B to A. Sew 2 pairs of squares together, carefully matching seams and fabrics for each half of the block. Sew the halves together to complete the design.

Outline-quilt the edges of each strip. For the ambitious quilter, add a single line of quilting across the middle of each strip.

EASY

Pieces per block: 24
A   4 dark I, 4 dark II
B   4 light, 4 medium
C   4 bright I, 4 bright II

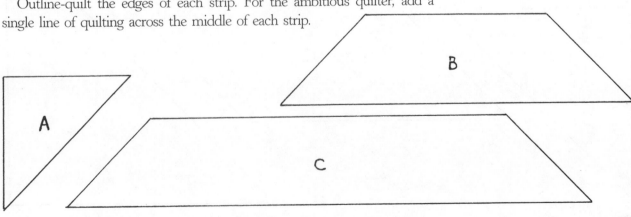

Spider

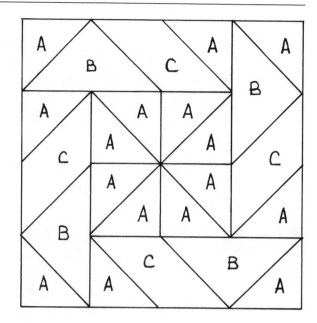

MODERATE

Pieces per block: 24
A   8 light, 8 dark
B   4 light
C   4 dark

Use highly contrasting fabrics to make this design vibrate with motion. Assemble the middle square first, then sew the outer strips around it. Sew 4 light A's to dark A's, making 4 squares. Sew the pairs of squares together, alternating fabrics, for each half of the central square. Sew the halves together, again alternating fabrics to create a pinwheel design. For each of the 4 strips, sew B to C, then sew a light and a dark A to each end as shown.

Following the diagram carefully, sew the first strip to the central square so that half of B extends beyond the corner of the middle. Working in a counterclockwise direction, sew the next 2 strips in place to the middle and to the previously sewn strip. Repeat for the final strip, angling your stitches sharply at the corner.

Outline-quilt all the dark pieces to delineate the spider. Quilt the light background pieces to create a web effect.

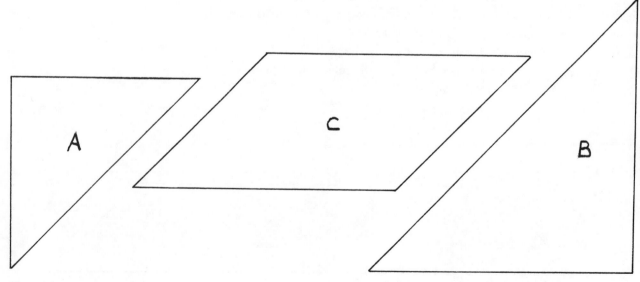

Spider Legs

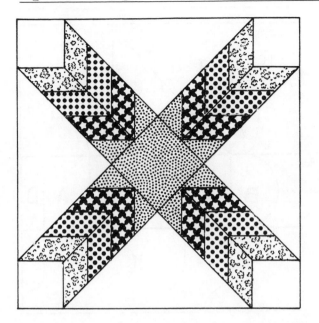
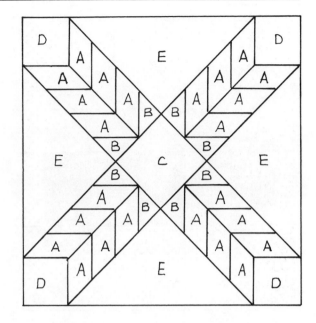

This block is challenging because some of the pieces must be inset into others; see How to Inset (page 15). Construct each of the 4 spider legs first. Then assemble the legs into 2 triangles that are sewn to each side of a central strip.

First, assemble the legs. Following the diagram carefully, sew 3 like A pieces together, forming a strip. In the same order and using the reversed A pieces, sew those 3 A's together, forming another strip. Sew a B to the end of each strip, then sew the strips together, matching seams carefully for the first leg. Repeat for the other legs.

Next, inset a D into the angle formed by each of the outer A pieces. Sew 2 leg pieces to each side of C for the central diagonal strip. Sew an E to each side of the remaining 2 legs to form the triangles. Sew a triangle to each side of the central strip to complete the design.

Outline-quilt each of the A and B pieces. Quilt a web design across the background D and E pieces.

CHALLENGING

Pieces per block: 41

A 4 bright I + 4 bright I reversed,
4 bright II + 4 bright II reversed,
4 dark + 4 dark reversed

B 4 medium + 4 medium reversed

C 1 medium

D 4 light

E 4 light

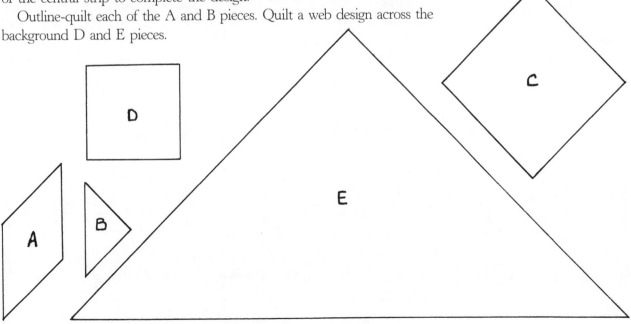

Bumblebee

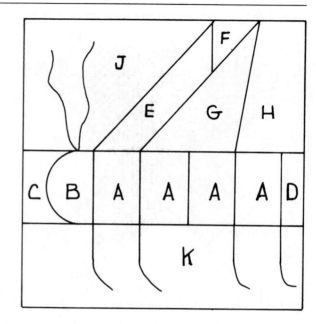

CHALLENGING

Pieces per block: 13

A 2 bright, 2 dark
B 1 dark
C 1 medium
D 1 medium
E 1 light reversed
F 1 medium reversed
G 1 light reversed
H 1 medium reversed
J 1 medium reversed
K 1 medium

This recognizable insect will delight children of both sexes. It requires some simple embroidery to delineate the antennae and legs.

For the body, sew the A's together, alternating bright and dark fabrics. Ease B into C; see Sewing Curves (page 16). Sew B to the bright A at one end; sew D to the dark A at the opposite end. For the wings, sew E to F as shown. Sew E-F to G, then sew H to the opposite side of G. Sew J to the remaining edge of E. Sew the wings to the body. Sew K to the opposite long edge of the body to complete the design.

Embroider the antennae and legs in outline stitch using black embroidery floss, following the dotted lines on the templates.

Outline-quilt the wings and each segment of the body.

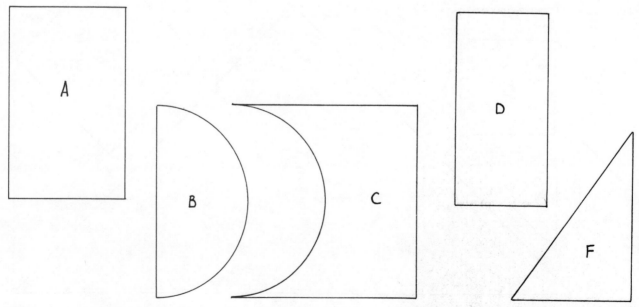

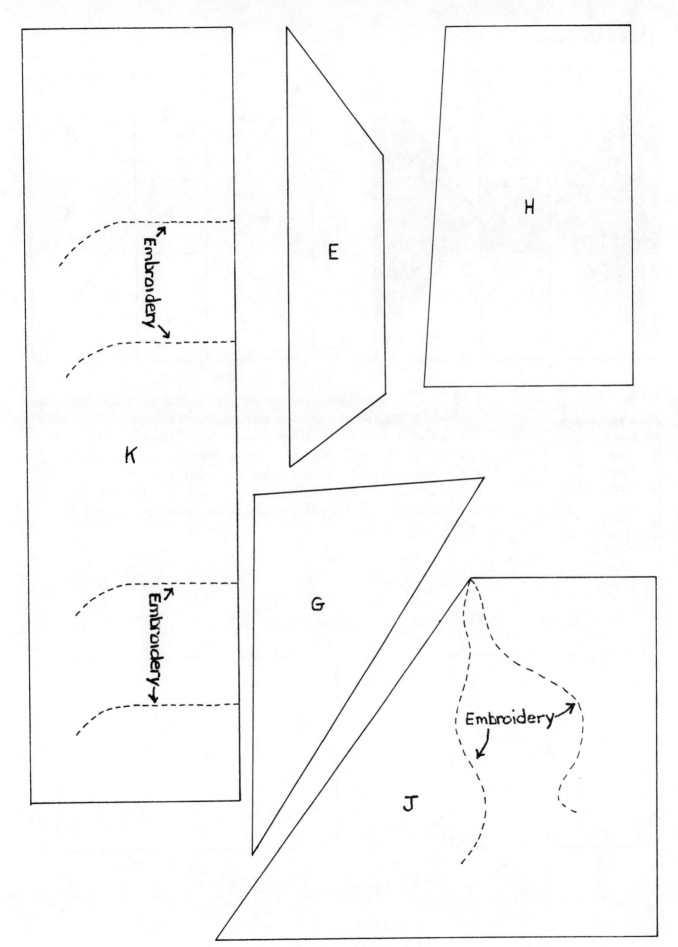

K

Embroidery

Embroidery

E

H

G

J

Embroidery

Bat's Wings

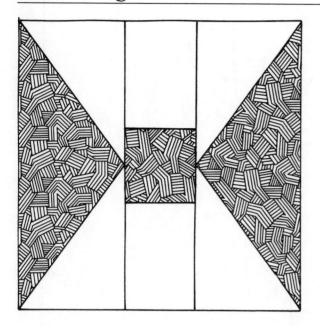
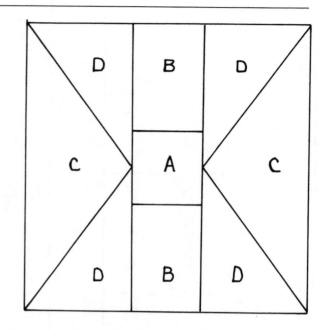

EASY

Pieces per block: 9

A 1 dark
B 2 light
C 2 dark
D 2 light + 2 light reversed

U se the darkest fabric in your quilt for the bat's wings and body. This dramatic design is quick to make in 3 vertical strips.

To begin, sew each B to opposite sides of A. Then sew a D to adjacent short edges of each C, being sure to use reversed pieces on each side. Sew D-C to each side of B-A-B to complete the design.

Quilt the bat's wings with concentric triangles and the body with concentric squares. Quilt a swirling cloud pattern across the background.

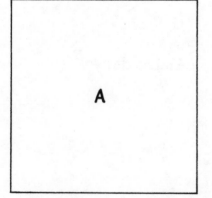

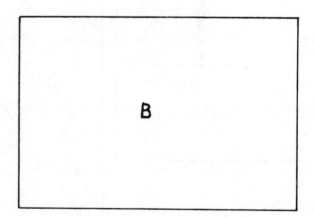

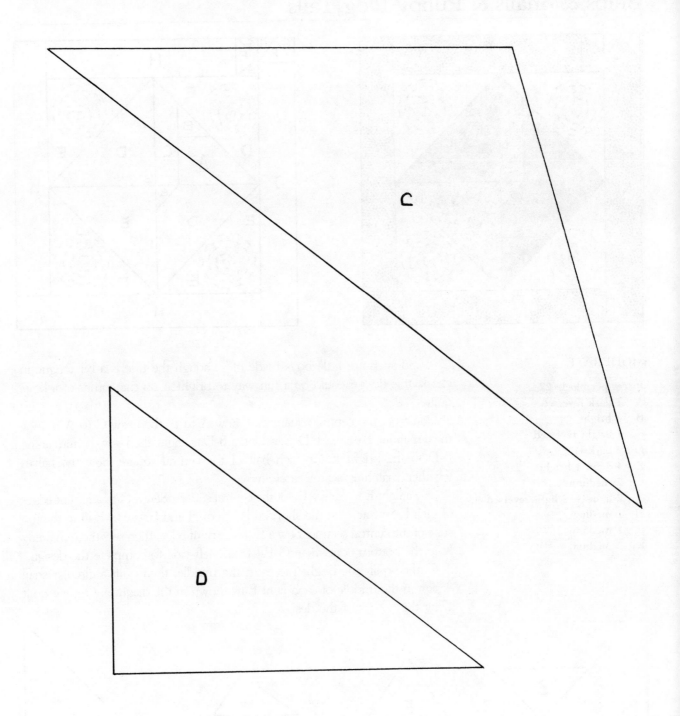

Snips & Snails & Puppy Dog Tails

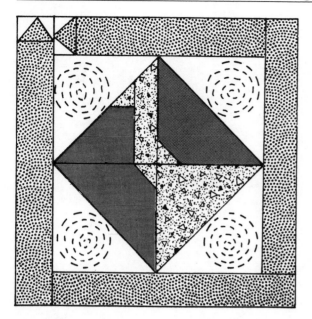

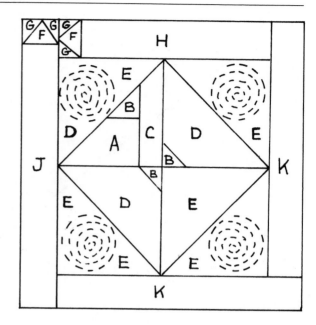

MODERATE

Pieces per block: 22

A	1 dark reversed
B	3 bright
C	1 bright reversed
D	2 dark
E	4 light, 1 bright
F	2 medium
G	2 light + 2 light reversed
H	1 medium
J	1 medium
K	2 medium

". . . and such are little boys made of." Though the title is a bit tongue in cheek, this design could be a fun way to brighten up the corner of a boy's quilt.

Construct the central square first. Sew A to B, then sew C to A-B. Sew the remaining B's to each D. Sew C to a B-D triangle, then sew the remaining B-D to the bright E for each half of the central square. Sew the halves together, matching seams carefully.

Sew a light E to each edge of the central square. Sew a G to adjacent edges of each F. Sew an F to the short end each of H and J. Sew G-F-H to the top edge of the central section. Sew a K to the right edge, then sew the remaining K to the bottom edge. Sew G-F-J to the left side to complete the design.

Outline-quilt the bright pieces in the middle, then quilt a circular snail design in the middle of each light E as shown in the diagram. Outline-quilt along the border of the design.

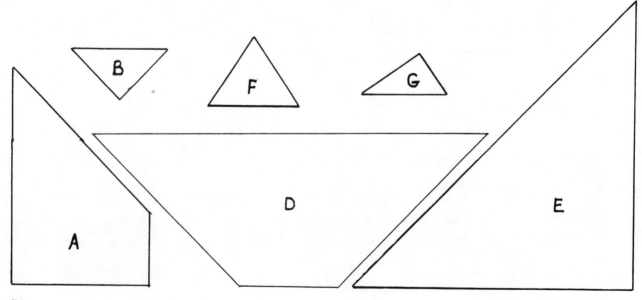

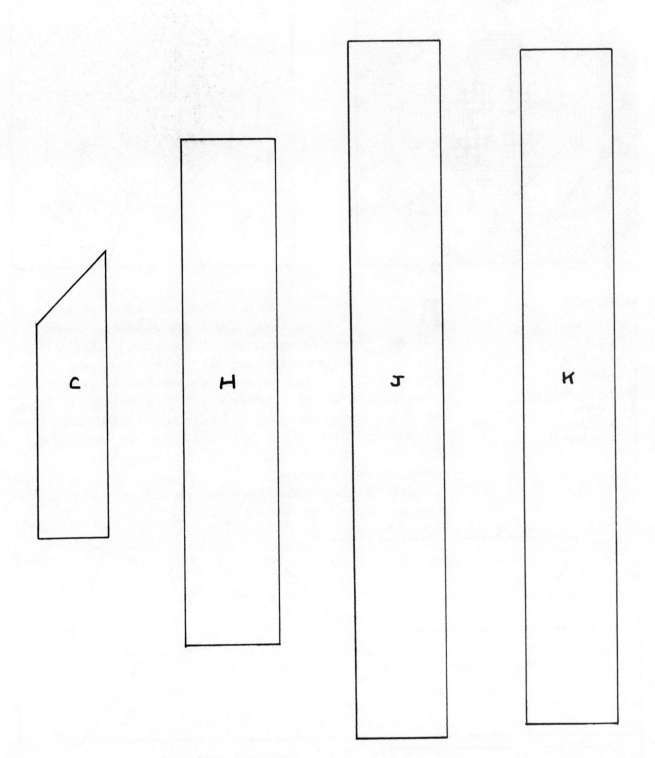

Spider Web

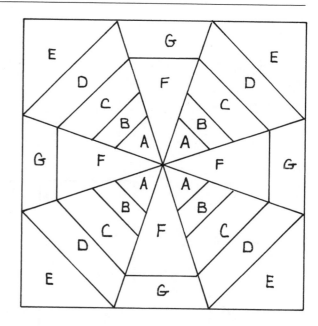

MODERATE

Pieces per block: 28

A   4 dark
B   4 medium I
C   4 light
D   4 medium II
E   4 bright
F   4 bright
G   4 medium II

Bold and bright—that's how this design looks when it is finished. It would be an excellent block to put in the middle of a boy's quilt.

To begin, construct each corner diamond. Sew A to B, B to C, C to D, and D to E. Next, assemble each triangle by sewing F to G. Sew a corner diamond to each side of a triangle, matching seams carefully; then arrange the remaining pieces on a flat surface with the completed edges at top and bottom. Sew a remaining triangle to the right side of the top and sew the other triangle to the left side of the bottom; this will form each half of the block. Sew the halves together, matching seams carefully, especially in the middle, to complete the design.

Quilt the design in concentric octagons to resemble a spider web. Quilt across the F pieces to continue the pattern.

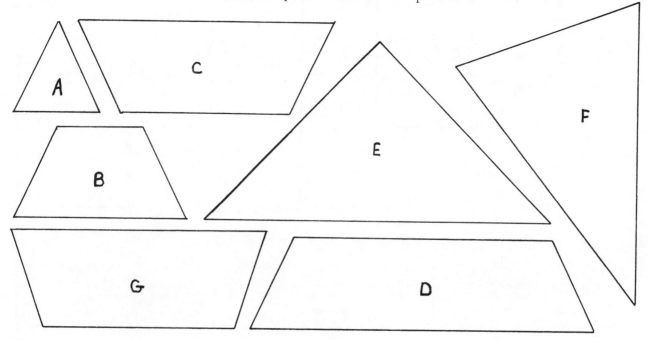

Snail Trail

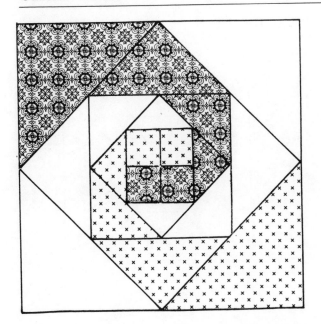
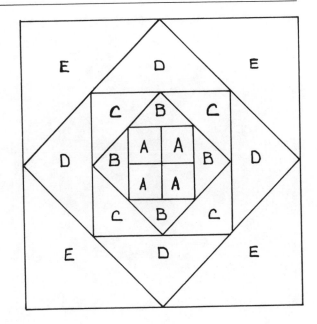

Discriminating use of fabric hues will dramatize this bold design. The block is constructed in concentric squares beginning in the middle. Follow the diagram carefully for fabric placement.

Sew the 4 A's together for the central square. Sew a B to each A-A edge. Sew a C to each B-B edge. Sew a D to each C-C edge. Sew an E to each D-D edge to complete the design.

Quilt the "snail trails" formed by the medium and dark fabrics and echo the quilting on the light fabric as well.

MODERATE

Pieces per block: 20

A   2 medium, 2 dark
B   2 light, 1 medium, 1 dark
C   2 light, 1 medium, 1 dark
D   2 light, 1 medium, 1 dark
E   2 light, 1 medium, 1 dark

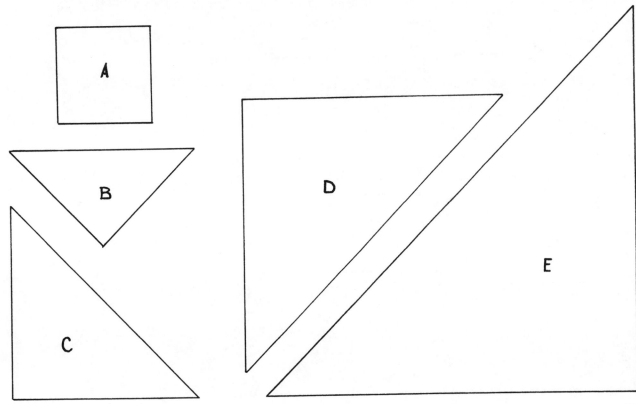

Snake Pit

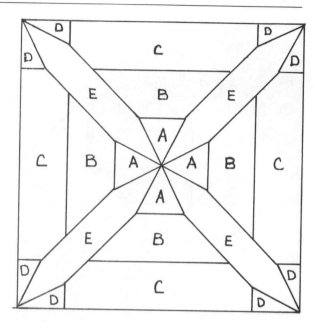

CHALLENGING

Pieces per block: 24

A   4 dark
B   4 bright
C   4 medium I
D   4 medium II + 4 medium
    II reversed
E   4 light

Snake Pit should be attempted only by experienced quilters who are proficient in sewing angled seams.

Assemble each of the 4 quarters of the pit first. Sew A to B and B to C. Then sew a D to each edge of C, using reversed D's to create the straight outer edge as shown in the diagram. Next, sew a pit quarter (A-B-C-D) to each side of 2 E's, angling your stitches at the corners of the E's. Sew an E to each free edge of the pit quarters on one half of the design, then sew the remaining pit half to the E's to complete the design.

Outline-quilt the snakes (E pieces), then quilt along each segment of the pit to create a sense of depth.

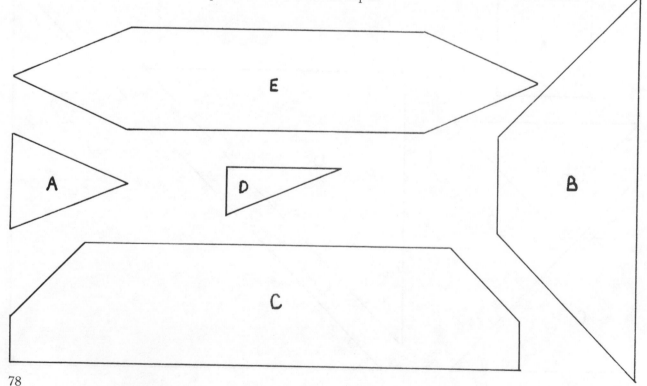

Flying Bat

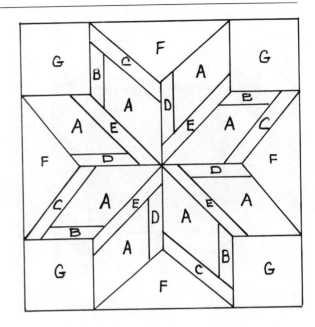

Though a bit tricky to assemble, Flying Bat is an exciting addition to any quilt. See How to Inset (page 15) before insetting around the edges.

To begin, assemble the pieces on a flat surface as shown in the diagram. Be careful not to mix up the B and D or C and E pieces. Sew B to A and D to A first. Then sew C to A-B and E to A-D as shown. Sew each D-E to A-C, forming 4 pairs of V-shaped pieces. Sew 2 pairs of V's together, forming each half of the middle. Press the middle seams of each half in opposite directions to reduce bulk. Sew the halves together, matching the seams in the middle. To complete the design inset the F and G pieces between the V's to form a square.

Outline-quilt the edge of the star and all of the light pieces.

CHALLENGING

Pieces per block: 32

A	8	medium
B	4	light
C	4	light
D	4	light
E	4	light
F	4	dark
G	4	dark

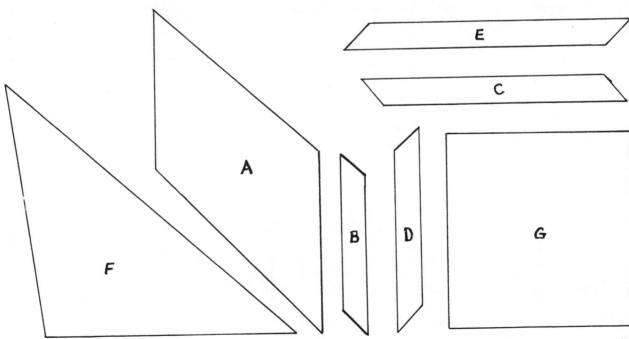

Toad in a Puddle

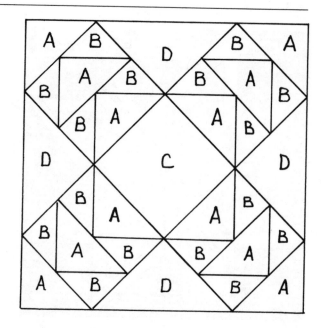

MODERATE

Pieces per block: 33

A   4 medium, 8 dark
B   16 light
C   1 medium
D   4 medium

A traditional and dramatic design, this will add a whimsical touch to any quilt. It is constructed in 2 triangles that are sewn to each side of a central diagonal strip.

To begin, sew a B to adjacent sides of each dark A. Following the diagram carefully, form 4 squares by sewing each B-B to an A. Sew a medium A to the top of each square as shown in the diagram. Sew the bottom of 2 of the pieces just made to opposite sides of C, making the central diagonal strip. Sew a D to each side of the remaining 2 pieces to make each triangle. Sew a triangle to each side of the central strip to complete the design.

Outline-quilt each dark A, then quilt a wave pattern across the background pieces.

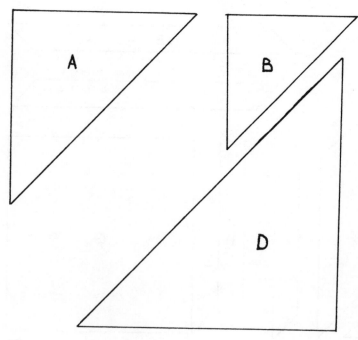

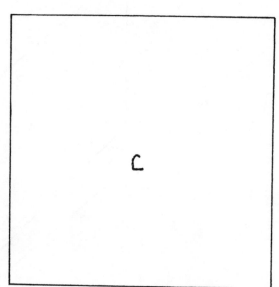

Flowers

Pocketful of Posies

(Color photos, pages D1 and E1)

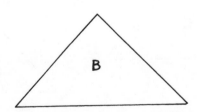

Although this block is made up of many pieces, the sewing is all straight and easy.

Arrange all of the pieces following the diagram. Sew all the pairs of B triangles together to form squares; press carefully. Put the B squares back into your arrangement, then assemble the block in 6 horizontal rows. Sew the rows to each other, matching seams carefully, to complete the design.

Quilt the block to emphasize each individual flower.

EASY

Pieces per block: 52

A 4 light, 4 bright I,
     8 bright II, 4 dark

B 4 light, 4 bright I, 8 bright
     II, 8 medium, 8 dark

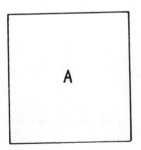

Circle of Irises

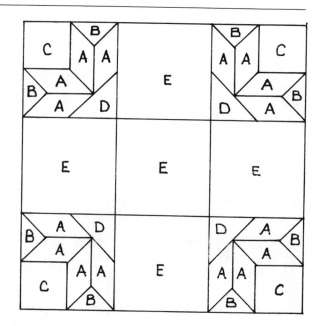

CHALLENGING

Pieces per block: 37

A 8 medium + 8 medium reversed

B 8 light

C 4 light

D 4 dark

E 4 light, 1 dark

This lovely design requires insetting 3 pieces into each of the 4 iris blocks; see How to Inset (page 15).

Construct the 4 iris blocks first. Sew the A's together to form the petals; inset the B and C pieces between the petals. Sew the D base to each flower. Join the flower blocks with the E blocks to form the design as shown in the diagram.

Quilt around each flower and the central square. Quilt a small flower in the middle of each E block.

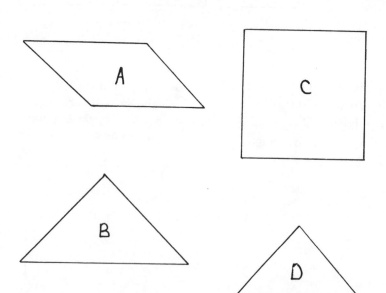
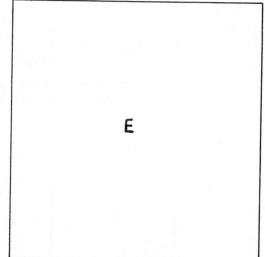

Circle of Rosebuds

(Color photo, page D1)

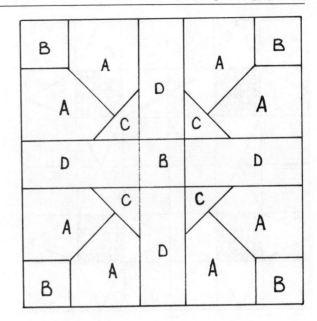

Insetting is necessary at each of this pretty design's corners; see How to Inset (page 15).

Construct each of the 4 rosebuds first. Sew each A to its reverse; inset B into each corner formed. Sew a C to the base of each flower. Form the top and bottom rows by sewing a rosebud square to each side of a D piece. Sew the remaining D's to each side of the dark B square. Connect the top and bottom rows by sewing to each side of the D-B-D strip.

Outline-quilt the design.

CHALLENGING

Pieces per block: 21

A   4 medium + 4 medium
      reversed
B   4 bright, 1 dark
C   4 dark
D   4 light

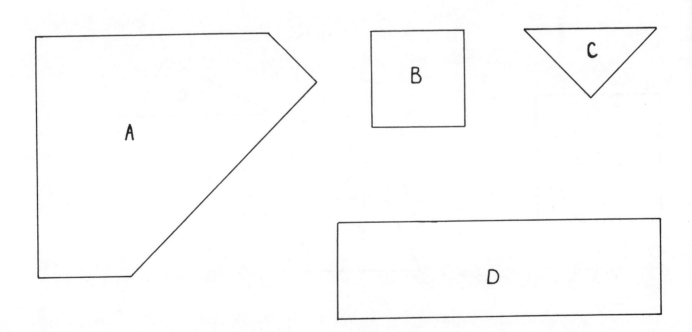

Daisy Ring

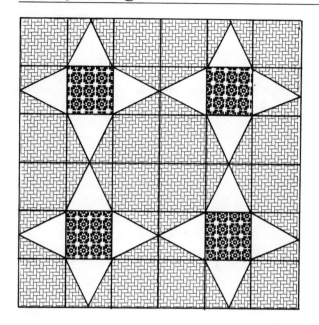

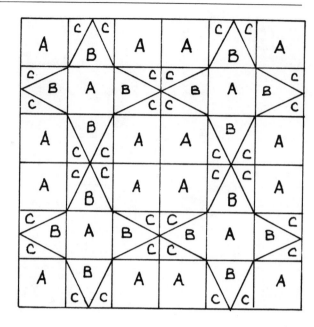

MODERATE

Pieces per block: 68

A   16 medium, 4 dark
B   16 light
C   16 medium + 16 medium
    reversed

Although this block has numerous pieces, it is easy to make and the finished "ring" effect is very pretty.

First, construct all the B-C squares, pressing carefully. Then arrange all the squares as shown in the diagram and assemble the block in 6 horizontal rows. Sew the rows to each other, matching seams carefully, to complete the design.

Outline-quilt each daisy and the edge of the block.

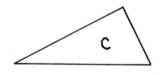

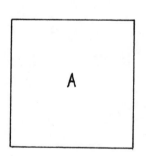

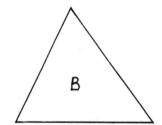

Dogwood Blossom

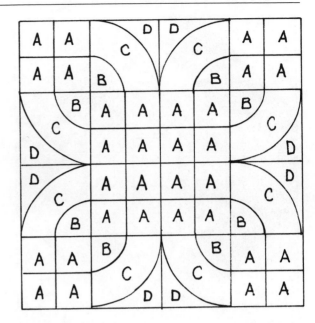

S ewing the curved pieces of this block is quite a challenge; see Sewing Curves (page 16).

Following the diagram, construct the 4-piece A squares. Make the B-C-D squares next by easing B into C, then easing C into D. Arrange the sewn squares as shown in the diagram and sew together in 4 horizontal rows. Sew the rows to each other, matching seams carefully, to complete the design.

Quilt the block to emphasize the curvilinear design.

CHALLENGING

Pieces per block: 56

A	16 light, 16 dark
B	8 light
C	8 medium
D	8 light

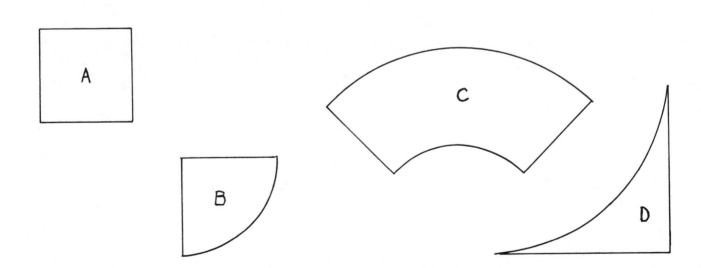

Floral Arrangement

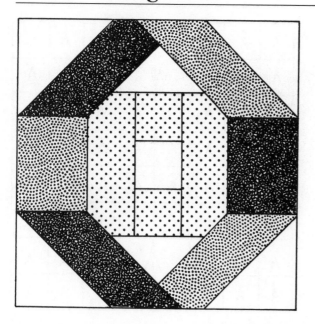

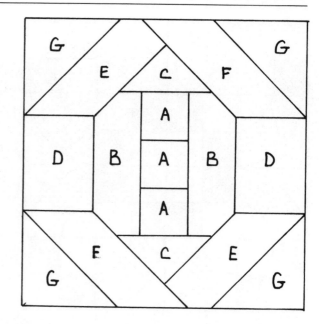

MODERATE

Pieces per block: 17

A	1 light, 2 bright
B	2 bright
C	2 light
D	1 medium, 1 dark
E	1 medium, 1 dark reversed
F	1 medium, 1 dark reversed
G	4 light

This appealing design is actually easier to construct than it appears to be. Use contrasting colors to create the illusion of depth in the ring around the flower.

Sew the 2 bright A's to each side of the light A. Sew a B to each side of the A strip to make the flower. Sew a C to the top and bottom of the flower. Sew a D to each side of the flower. Sew an E to each side corner of the central square, turning your stitching at the B-D seam. In the same manner, sew an F to the remaining side corners of the middle. Complete the design by sewing a G in each corner.

Outline-quilt the design to emphasize the flower and the ring around it.

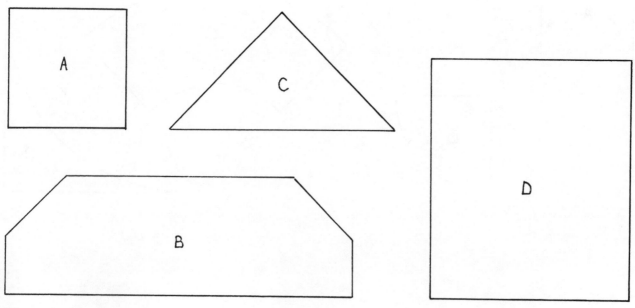

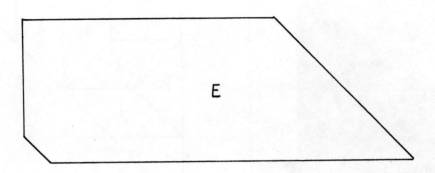

E

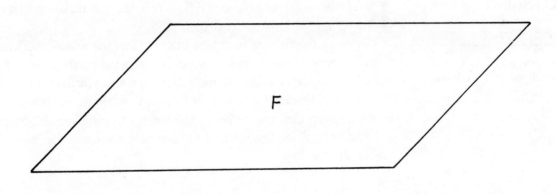

F

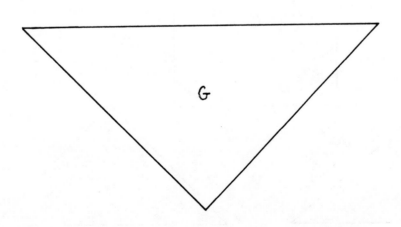

G

Flower Pot

(Color photo, page D1)

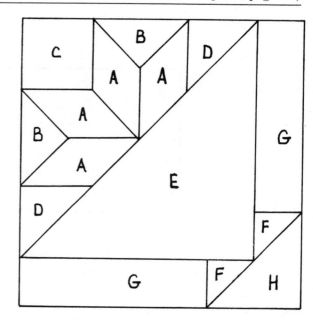

CHALLENGING

Pieces per block: 15

A 1 bright + 1 bright
   reversed,
   1 medium + 1 medium
   reversed
B 2 light
C 1 light
D 2 light
E 1 dark
F 2 dark
G 2 light
H 1 light

Required insetting around the flowers in the pot makes this block challenging; see How to Inset (page 15).

Construct the flowers first. Sew bright A's to the reverse medium A's to form the petals; inset B and C pieces between the petals. Sew a D to each side of the flower, creating a triangle. Next, construct the basket by sewing an F to the end of each G; sew each F-G to E as shown, then sew H to the bottom corner. Sew the basket to the flowers to complete the design.

Quilt around the flowers and the basket. Crosshatch the interior of the basket with quilting.

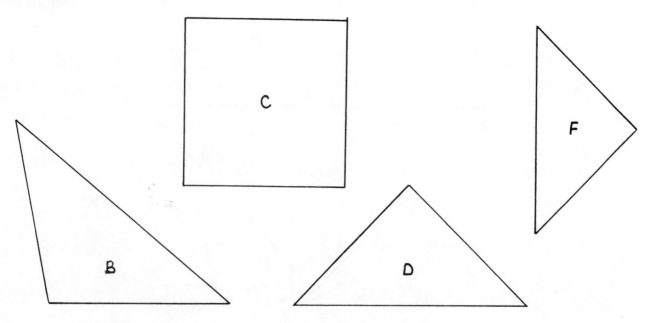

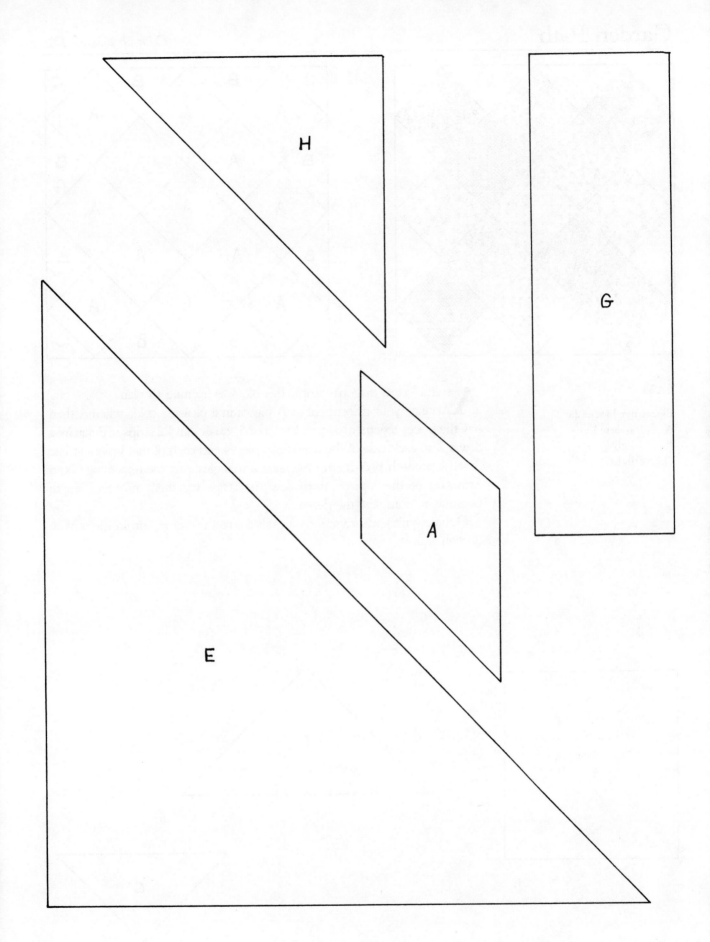

Garden Path

(Color photo, page D1)

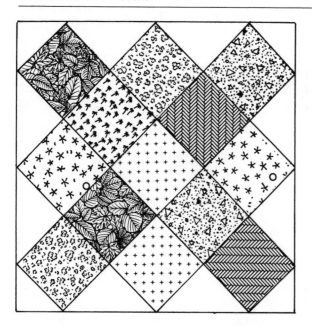

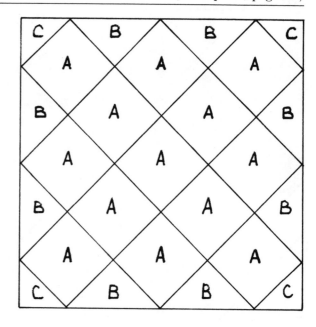

EASY

Pieces per block: 25
A   13 assorted
B   8 light
C   4 light

Assembled in diagonal strips, this block is exciting to plan. Arrange your assortment of A pieces in a pleasing color scheme, then sew the pieces together to form 1 strip of 5 squares and 2 strips of 3 squares. Sew a B to each side of the 2 single A pieces and each of the 3-piece strips. Sew a C to each B-A-B strip to create 2 triangles; sew the remaining C's to each end of the 5-piece strip. Sew the strips together, matching seams carefully, to complete the design.

Outline-quilt each square, then quilt a small flower design in the middle of each square.

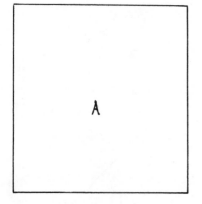

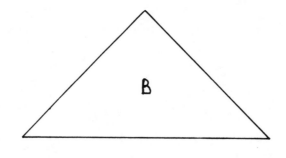

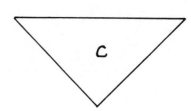

Pansy

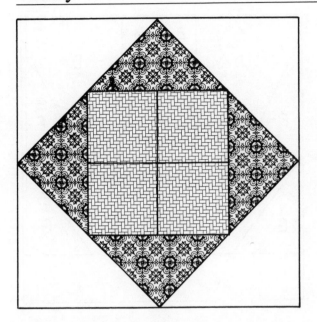

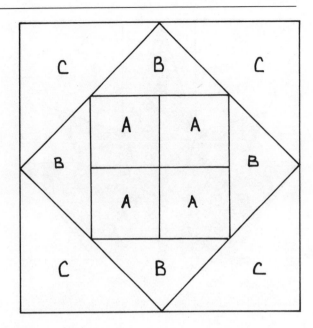

This block is very quick and easy to make. Just remember when choosing your colors that the B pieces represent the petals.

Sew the 4 A's together to form a large square. Sew a B to each edge of the square. Sew a C to each corner to complete the design.

Quilt the block to emphasize the petals and the A pieces of the pansy.

EASY

Pieces per block: 12
A   4 medium
B   4 dark
C   4 light

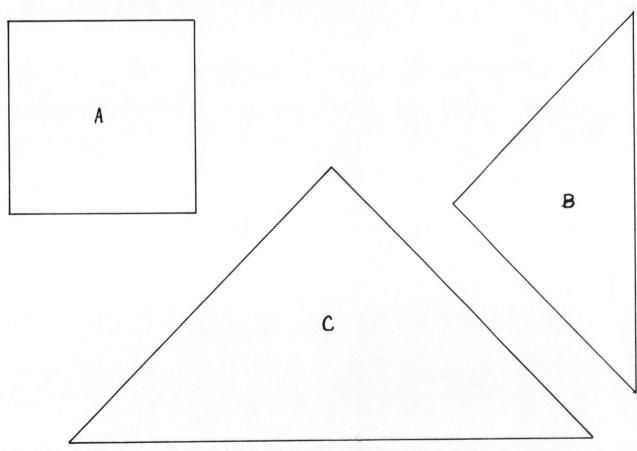

91

Water Lily

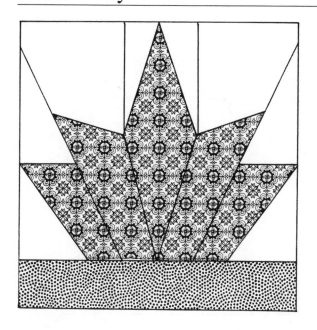

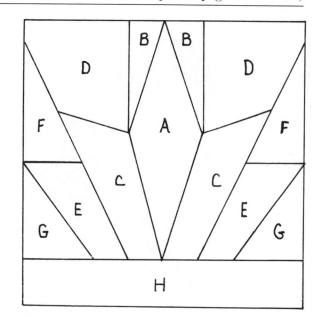

MODERATE

Pieces per block: 14

A 1 bright

B 1 light + 1 light reversed

C 1 bright + 1 bright reversed

D 1 light + 1 light reversed

E 1 bright + 1 bright reversed

F 1 light + 1 light reversed

G 1 light + 1 light reversed

H 1 medium

This outstanding design would look wonderful in a central position on a sampler quilt.

Sew a B to each side of A. Sew a D to the top of each C. Sew C-D to A-B, turning stitching slightly at the corner of A on each side. Sew an F to each E. Sew a G to each E. Sew E-F-G to each side of the middle. Sew H to the bottom of the water lily to complete the design.

Quilt around the edge of each petal and the lily pad.

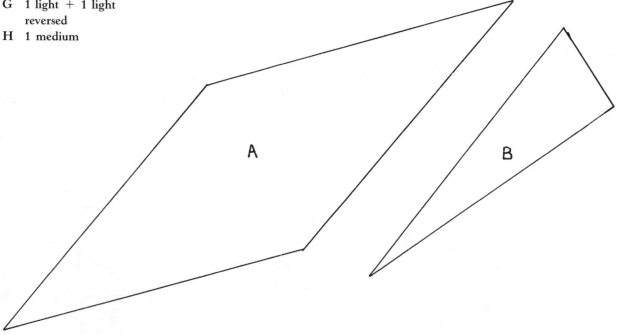

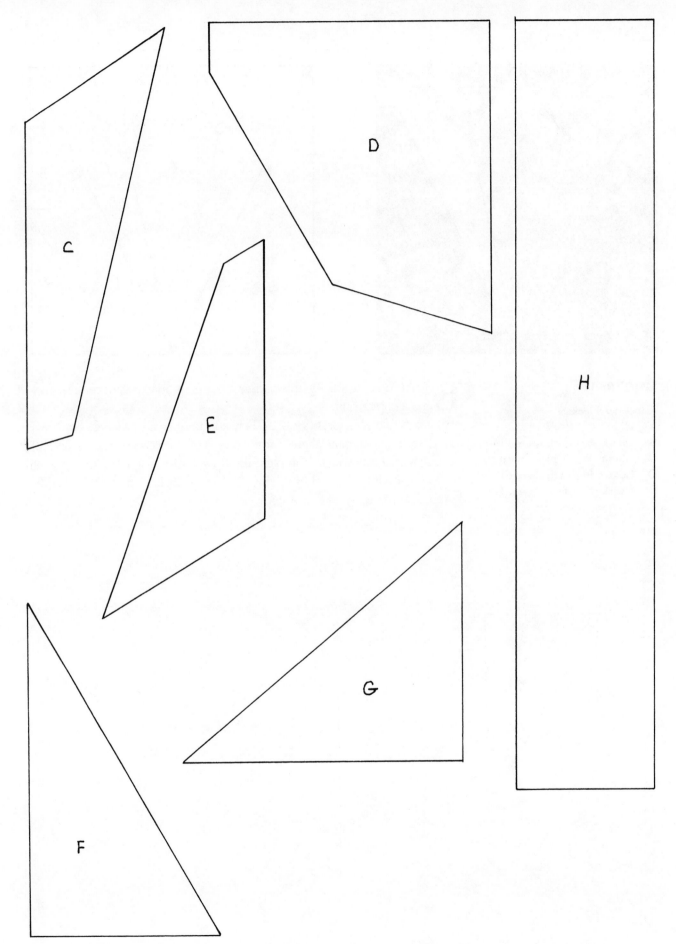

Lily

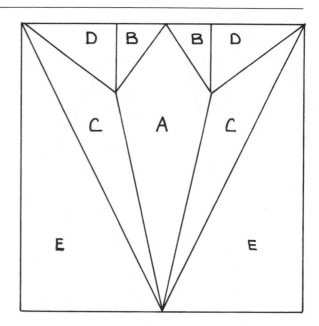

MODERATE

Pieces per block: 9

A   1 light
B   1 dark + 1 dark reversed
C   1 light + 1 light reversed
D   1 dark + 1 dark reversed
E   1 dark + 1 dark reversed

Elegant in its simplicity, this dramatic design is an excellent central block in a sampler quilt.

Sew a B to each short edge of A. Sew a D to the top of each C. Sew C-D to A-B, turning stitching slightly at the corner of A on each side. Sew an E to each side of the flower to complete the design.

Outline-quilt each petal of the lily. Quilt straight lines radiating from the flower towards each edge of the block.

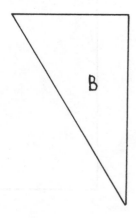

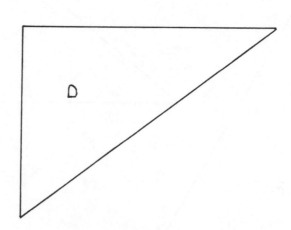

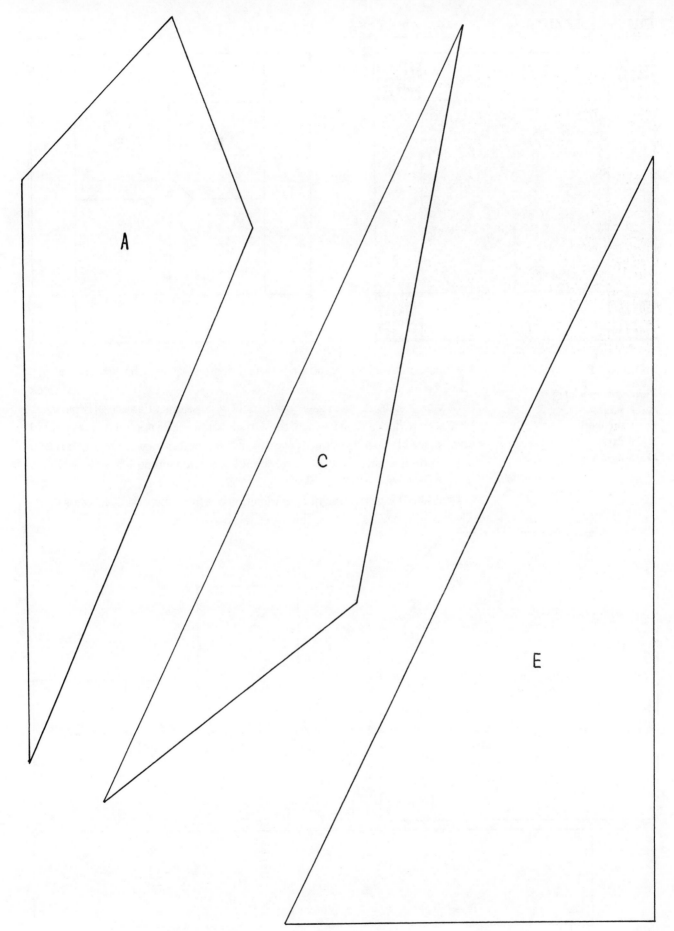

Busy Lizzie

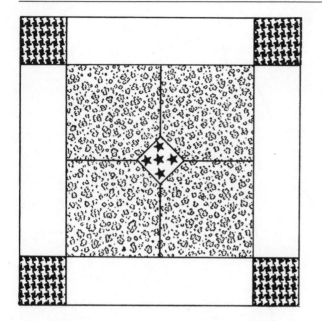

MODERATE

Pieces per block: 13
- A 1 bright
- B 4 medium
- C 4 dark
- D 4 light

This design is composed of a pieced central square (the flower) and a border.

Sew each B to A, then sew together the side seams of adjacent B pieces. Or you may find it easier to sew the 4 B's together, then appliqué A over the middle; see How to Appliqué (page 16). For the border, sew a D to each side of the central square. Sew a C to each end of the remaining D's; sew C-D to the top and bottom of the block to complete the design.

Quilt the flower in straight lines radiating out from the middle towards the edges of the petals; then outline-quilt the border pieces.

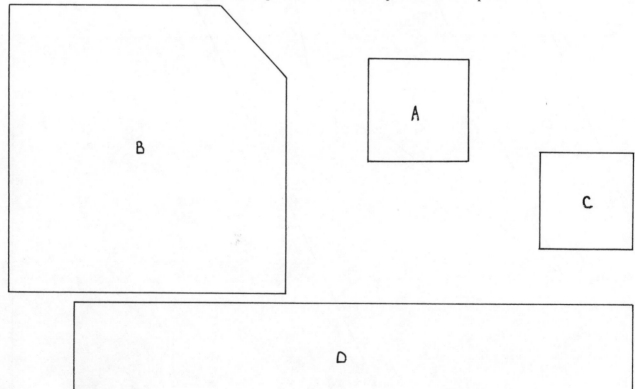

Bouquet in a Fan

(Color photos, pages D1 and E4)

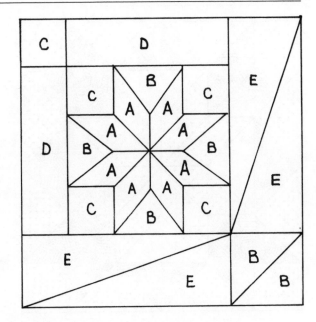

This pretty design requires accurate cutting and piecing to accentuate the flower points. Insetting is done at each edge of the flower; see How to Inset (page 15).

Sew each A to its reverse template, forming 4 pairs of flower petals. Sew 2 pairs of petals together, forming each half of the flower; press the seams of each half in opposite directions to reduce bulk in the middle. Sew the halves of the flower together, matching the seams in the middle. Inset the B and C pieces between the petals to form a square. Sew a D to one side of the flower square; sew C to D, then sew to top of the square as shown.

To form the fan, sew together medium and dark B pieces and E pieces. Sew 1 E rectangle to the base of the flower square as shown. Sew the B square to the end of the remaining E rectangle; sew E-B to the side of the block to complete the design.

Outline-quilt the flower and the fan.

CHALLENGING

Pieces per block: 25
A   4 light + 4 light reversed
B   5 medium, 1 dark
C   5 medium
D   2 medium
E   2 medium, 2 dark

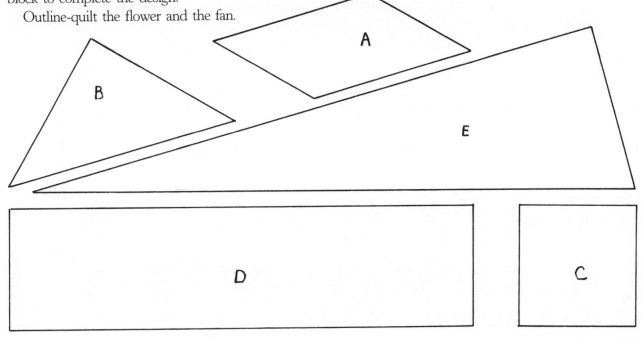

Aster

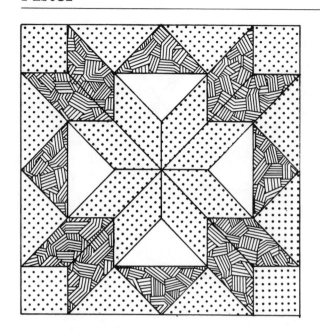

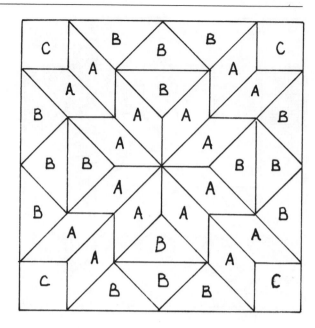

CHALLENGING

Pieces per block: 36

A 4 medium + 4 medium
      reversed,
      4 dark + 4 dark reversed
B 4 light, 8 medium, 4 dark
C 4 medium

This block is challenging because some of the pieces must be inset into each other; see How to Inset (page 15).

Begin construction of the central flower by sewing each medium A to its matching dark A, forming 8 long A strips. Next, sew each A strip to its reverse, forming 4 pairs of flower petals. Sew 2 pairs of petals together along the medium A edges, forming each half of the flower; press the seams of each half in opposite directions to reduce bulk in the middle. Sew the halves of the flower together, matching the central seams. Inset the C pieces between the petals to square the corners.

Make 4 large triangles by sewing the B's together as shown in the diagram. Inset one large B triangle into each side of the flower, matching seams carefully.

Quilt around the central portion of the flower to give it prominence, then outline-quilt all the other pieces.

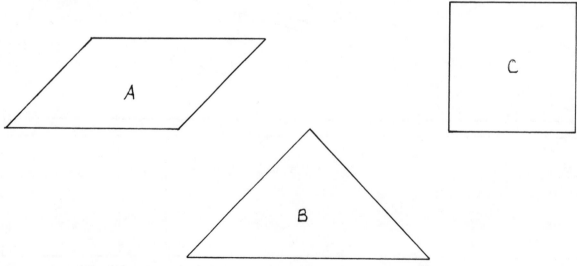

Rosebud

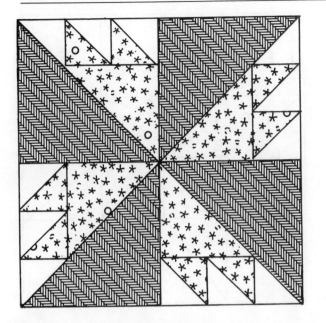
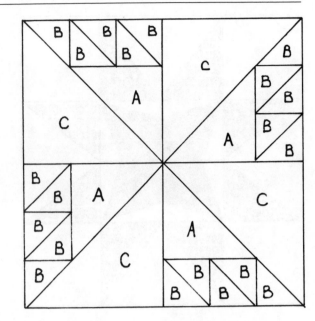

The his design is easily constructed from 4 pieced squares.
Sew the B triangles together alternately to form 4 strips with 5 triangles in each strip as shown in the diagram. Sew each B strip to an A. Sew each A-B to C, forming 4 squares. Sew 2 pairs of squares together, making each half of the block. Sew the halves together, matching seams carefully, to complete the design.

Outline-quilt each rosebud; quilt a small flower in the middle of each C piece.

EASY

Pieces per block: 28
A   4 medium
B   12 light, 8 medium
C   4 dark

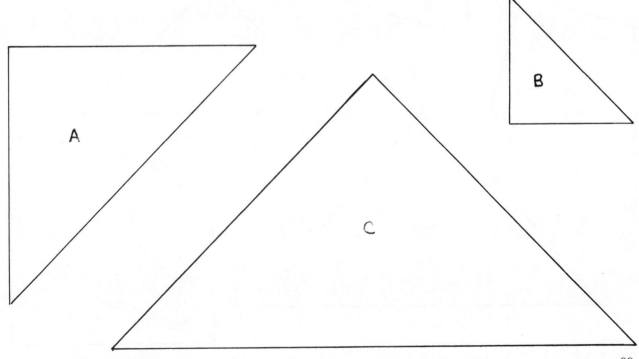

Starflower

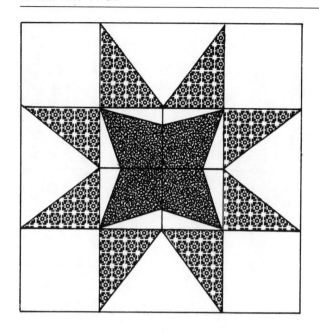

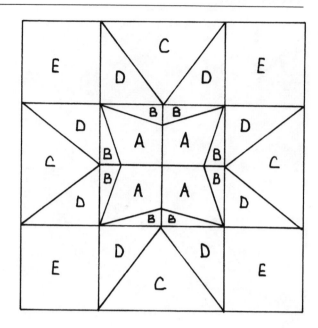

MODERATE

Pieces per block: 28

A 4 dark
B 4 light + 4 light reversed
C 4 light
D 8 medium
E 4 light

Whe n constructed accurately this design can be very beautiful; take care to cut and piece carefully.

Sew a B to each long edge of each A, forming 4 squares. Sew the squares together as shown in the diagram to create the flower heart. Sew a D to each side of C, forming 4 rectangles. Sew a D-C-D rectangle to each side of the central square. Sew an E to each side of the remaining D-C-D rectangles. Sew the strips just made to the top and bottom to complete the block.

Outline-quilt the outer edges and the heart of the starflower.

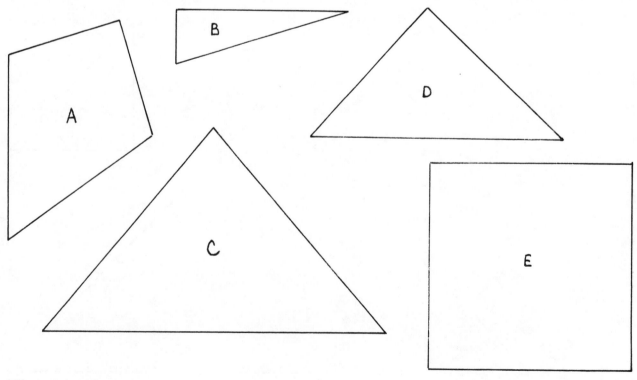

Sunflower

(Color photo, page D1)

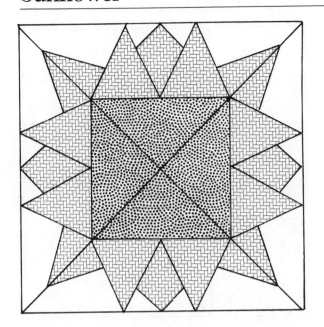

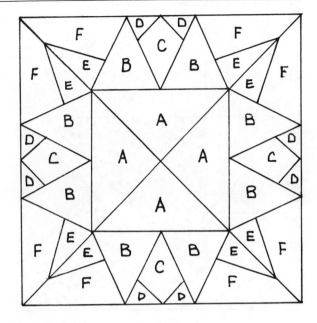

Use a stripe for the medium fabric to create an interesting petal effect as shown in the color photograph of the Flowers quilt (page D1). Study the diagram carefully. You'll see that the design is made up of 4 large triangles. Each triangle is constructed separately, then the 4 are joined to create the complete sunflower.

To begin, sew a D to each short edge of C, forming a small triangle. Sew a B to each side of C-D. Sew E to F, forming another triangle; repeat with reversed E and F pieces. Sew an E-F triangle to each side of B. Sew this pieced strip to the long edge of A, forming a large triangle, one quarter of the block. Repeat for the other three quarters. Sew the quarters together to form halves; sew the halves together to complete the design.

Quilt the block to emphasize each petal and the middle.

CHALLENGING

Pieces per block: 40

A 4 dark
B 8 medium
C 4 medium
D 4 light + 4 light reversed
E 4 medium + 4 medium reversed
F 4 light + 4 light reversed

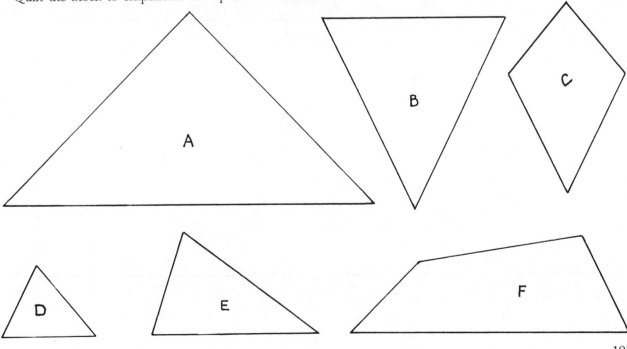

101

Cactus Flower

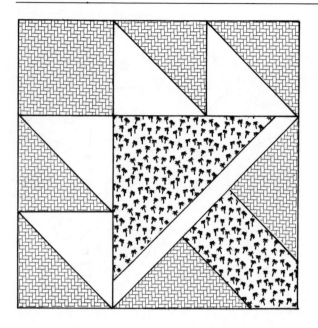

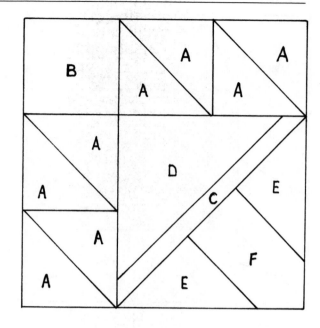

EASY

Pieces per block: 14

A 4 light, 4 medium
B 1 medium
C 1 light
D 1 bright
E 2 medium
F 1 bright

Very quick and easy to construct, this design consists of a pieced square with a border on 2 sides.

Sew the light and medium A pieces together, making 4 squares. Sew 2 A squares together for the side, then sew 2 A squares to each other and to a B square for the top border strip. Sew C to D. Sew the side A strip to C-D. Sew the top A-B strip to C-D. Sew an E to each side of F; sew E-F to C to complete the design.

Outline-quilt the cactus flower.

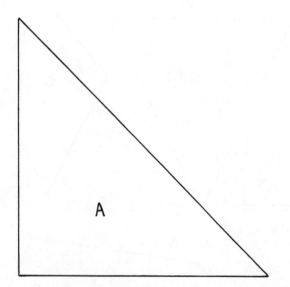

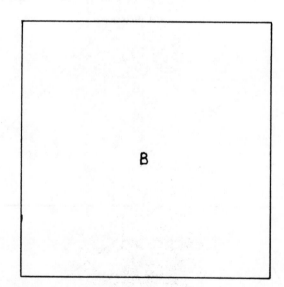

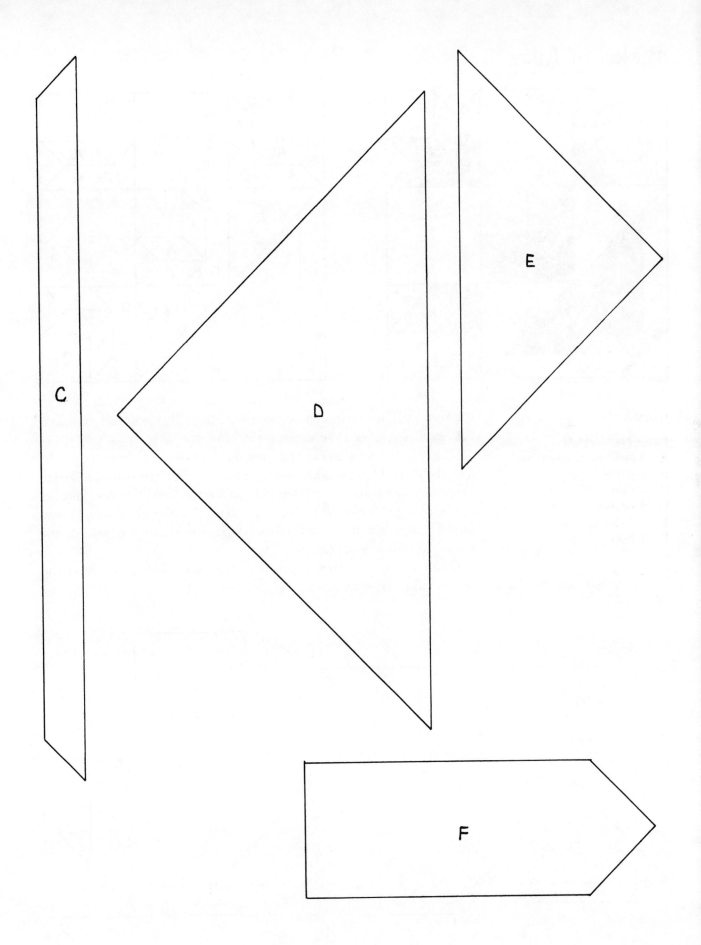

Basket of Lilies

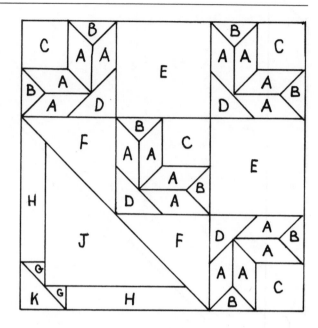

CHALLENGING

Pieces per block: 42

A	8 medium + 8 medium reversed
B	8 light
C	4 light
D	4 dark
E	2 light
F	2 light
G	2 dark
H	1 light + 1 light reversed
J	1 dark
K	1 light

This design is a bit of a challenge because the 4 lily blocks each contain 3 inset pieces; see How to Inset (page 15).

Construct the 4 lily blocks first. Sew the A's together to form the petals; inset the B and C pieces between the petals. Sew the D base to each flower. Form the upper portion of the design by sewing the E and F pieces to the lily blocks. Next, construct the basket by sewing a G to the end of each H; sew G-H to J as shown, then sew K to the bottom corner. Sew the basket to the flowers to complete the design.

Quilt around each complete flower and around the basket. Crosshatch the interior of the basket with quilting.

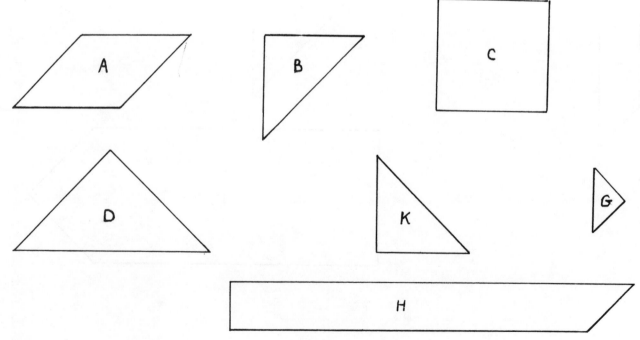

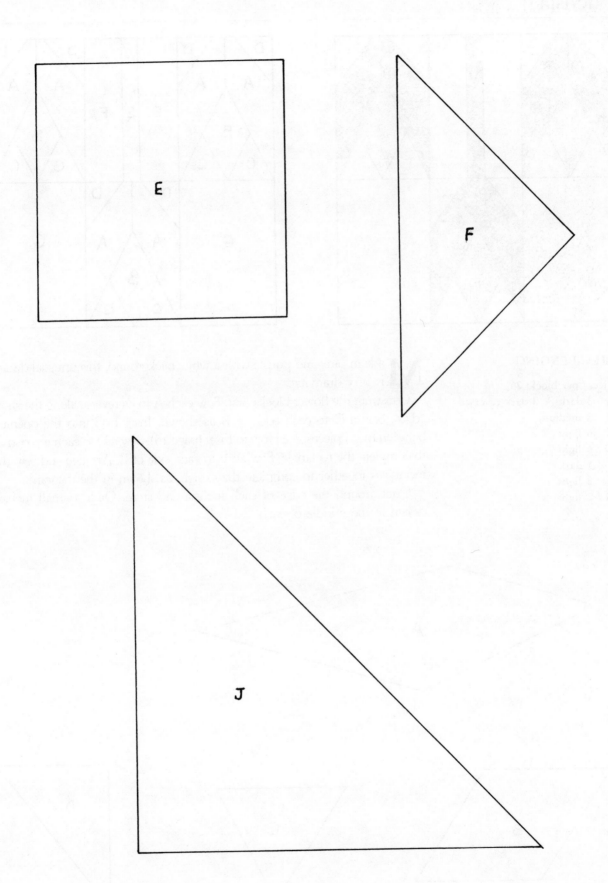

Fuchsia

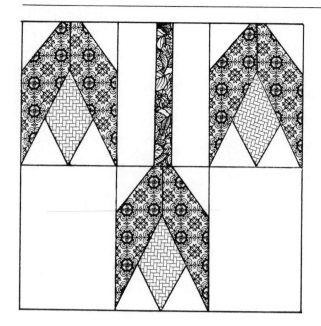

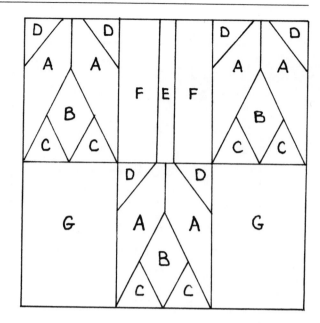

CHALLENGING

Pieces per block: 26

A   3 dark + 3 dark reversed
B   3 medium
C   6 light
D   6 light
E   1 dark
F   2 light
G   2 light

Made in pink and purple with a white background, this unusual design is very dramatic.

Construct the flower blocks first. Sew each A to its reverse along the short edges. Sew a C to each edge of B as shown. Inset B-C into the opening between the A pieces; see How to Inset (page 15). Sew a D to each top corner to complete the rectangle. Sew an F to each side of E. Arrange and sew the rectangles together to complete the design, as shown in the diagram.

Quilt around the edge of each fuchsia and stem. Quilt a small fuchsia design in the middle of each G block.

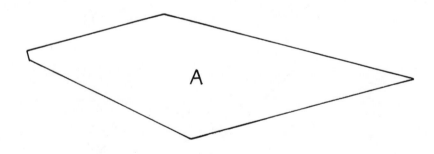

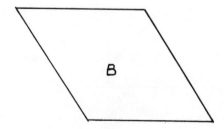

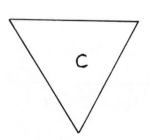

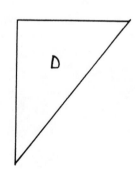

E

F

G

Nosegay

(Color photos, pages D1 and E3)

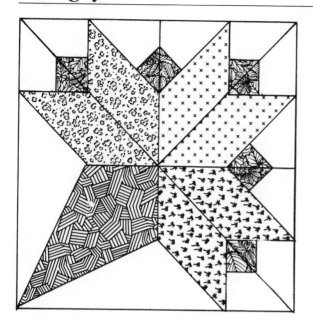

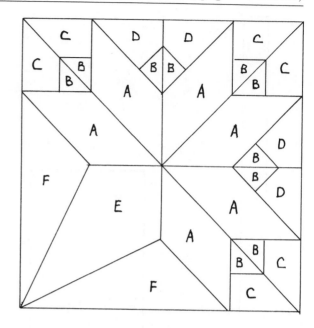

MODERATE

Pieces per block: 29

A   1 bright + 1 bright
    reversed,
    1 medium I + 1 medium I
    reversed,
    1 medium II + 1 medium
    II reversed
B   10 dark I
C   3 light + 3 light reversed
D   2 light + 2 light reversed
E   1 dark II
F   1 light + 1 light reversed

S tudy the diagram. You'll see that the block is made of 2 large right-angled triangles; the triangles are sewn together to complete the design.

First, sew a B to each C and D, creating a series of triangles. Arrange the A petals in the order that you want them to appear. Next, arrange the appropriate B-C or B-D triangles in place next to the A petals; sew 1 triangle to each petal. Sew the 4 inner petal pieces together, matching seams carefully, to form half of the block. Sew the 2 outer petal pieces to each short edge of E. Inset an F into each opening to complete the other half of the block. Sew the 2 halves together, matching seams carefully, to complete the design.

Quilt around each petal and the handle of the nosegay.

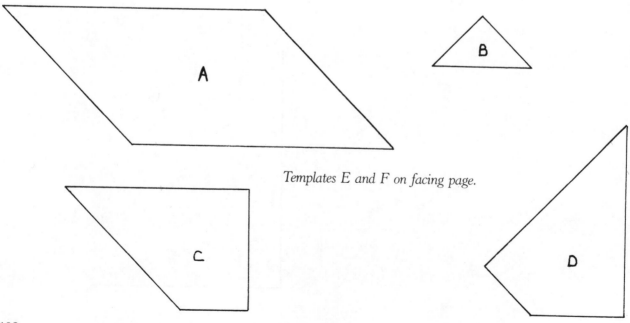

Templates E and F on facing page.

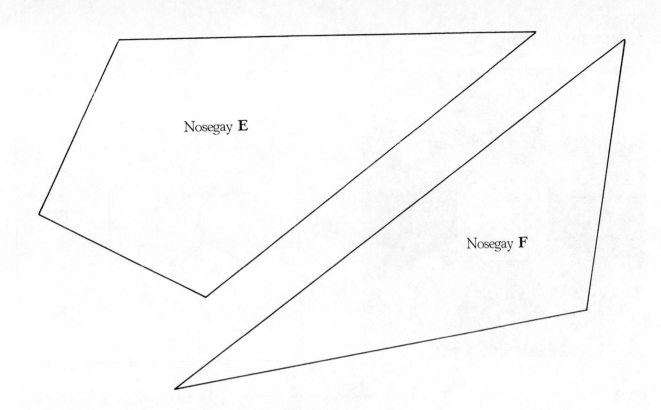

Nosegay **E**

Nosegay **F**

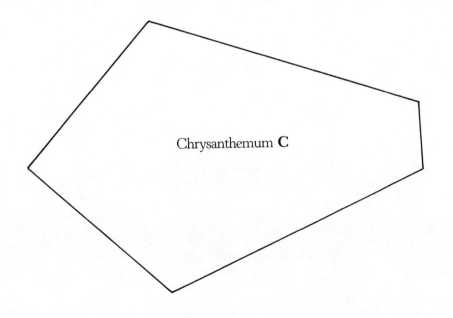

Chrysanthemum **C**

Chrysanthemum

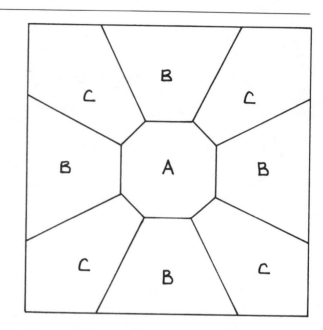

EASY

Pieces per block: 9
A   1 light
B   4 dark
C   4 medium

You can completely piece this design, but it is much quicker and easier to appliqué the middle piece in place; see How to Appliqué (page 16).

Sew the B and C pieces together alternately to form the outer portion of the square. Appliqué A over the central opening.

Quilt each petal of the flower with half circles radiating outward from the middle.

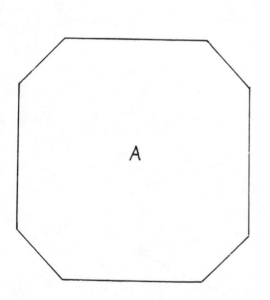

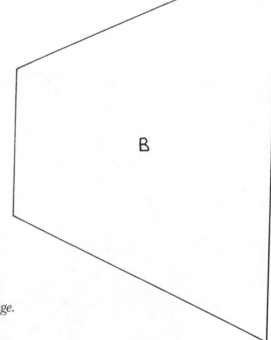

Template C on preceding page.

Four-Leaf Clover

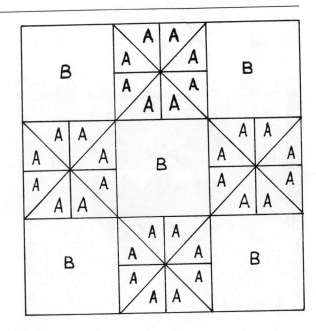

EASY

Pieces per block: 37
A 16 light, 16 medium
B 5 medium

This simple design adds sparkle to any corner of a sampler quilt. Construct each of the four-leaf clover blocks first. Sew together the light and medium A's to form small squares. Sew the squares together as shown to complete each four-leaf clover. Following the diagram, join the clover squares with the B's in 3 horizontal rows. Then sew the rows together to complete the design.

Quilt around the light triangles, then quilt a small four-leaf clover in the middle of each B square.

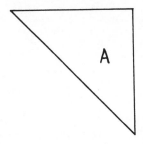

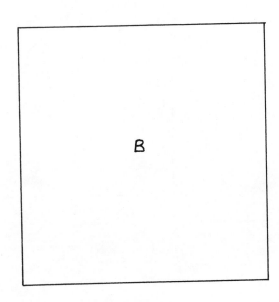

Tulip Garden

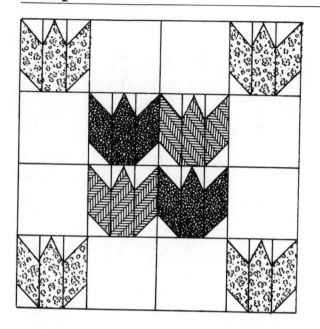
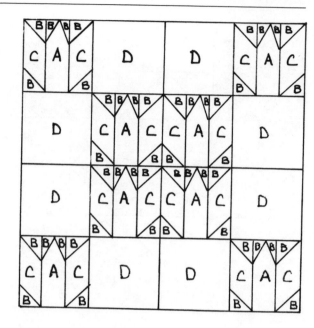

CHALLENGING

Pieces per block: 80
- **A**   4 bright, 2 medium, 2 dark
- **B**   48 light
- **C**   4 bright + 4 bright reversed,
     2 medium + 2 medium reversed,
     2 dark + 2 dark reversed
- **D**   8 light

This block will probably take a lot of time to cut and piece, but it will look striking in a sampler quilt (where you only have to make it once!).

Assemble all the tulip squares first. Sew a B to each angled edge of each A. Sew a B to each angled edge of each C. Sew a B-C strip to each side of each A-B strip. Assemble the tulip blocks with the D squares following the diagram; sew to form 4 horizontal rows. Sew the rows together, matching seams carefully, to complete the design.

Outline-quilt each tulip. Quilt a tulip in the middle of each D piece.

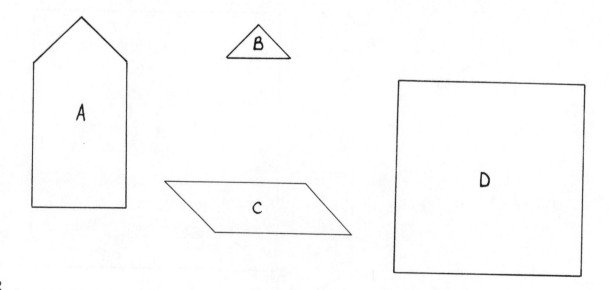

Sugar & Spice
& All Things Nice

Let Me Call You Sweetheart

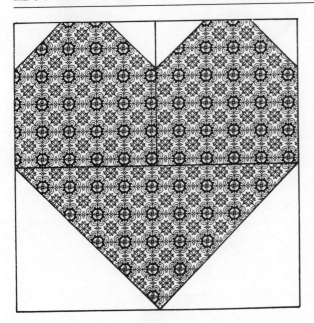

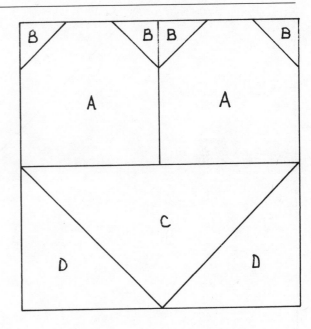

Little girls love hearts and flowers. Easily recognizable, this design will surely charm a female of any age.

Sew a B to each angled edge of A. Sew A-B together as shown for the top of the heart. Sew a D to each short edge of C for the bottom of the heart. Sew the top to the bottom to complete the design.

Quilt small heart shapes at random all across the block, ignoring the seams.

EASY

Pieces per block: 9

A	2	dark
B	4	light
C	1	dark
D	2	light

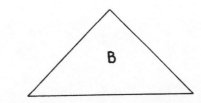

Templates A, C and D on following page.

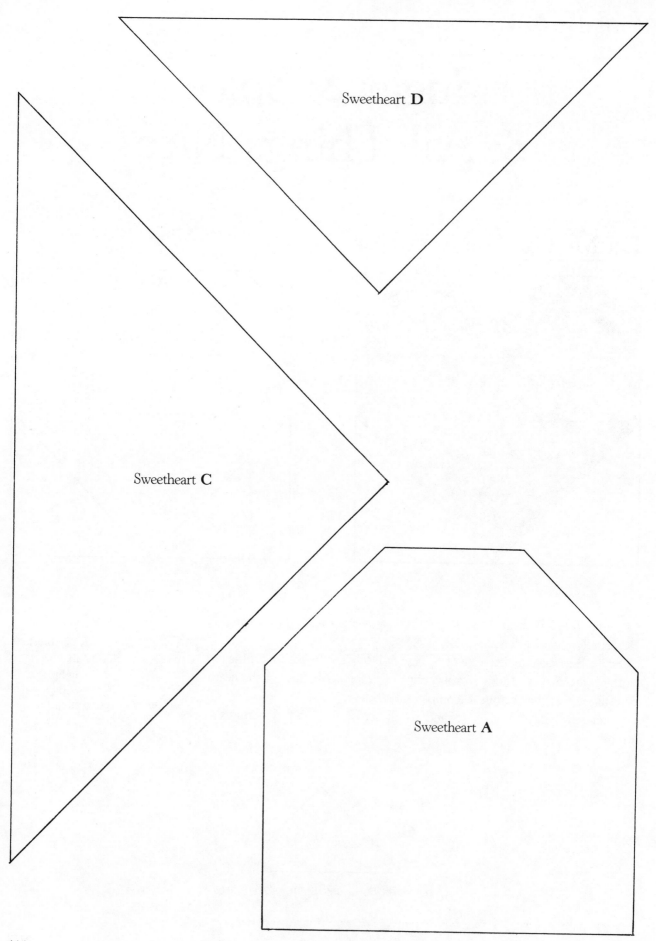

Sweetheart **D**

Sweetheart **C**

Sweetheart **A**

Birthday Cake

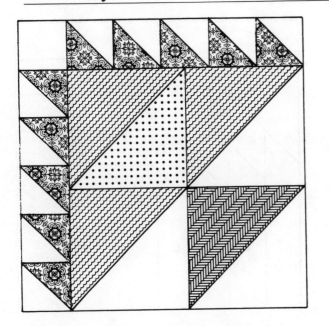

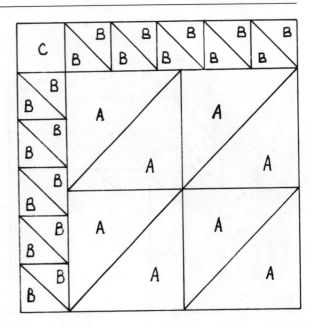

This design would be appropriate for a quilt you make to present on a child's birthday.

First, assemble the cake by sewing a medium A to each edge of the bright A. Next, assemble the base by sewing a light A to each edge of the dark A. Sew the base to the cake. Next, construct the candles by sewing a light B to each dark B. Sew 5 sets of B squares together to make the 2 border strips. Sew 1 strip to the side of the cake. Sew a C to the left end of the remaining strip and sew to the top of the block to complete the design.

Quilt along each seam of the cake, stand and candles.

MODERATE

Pieces per block: 29

A   3 light, 1 bright II,
     3 medium, 1 dark
B   10 light, 10 bright I
C   1 light

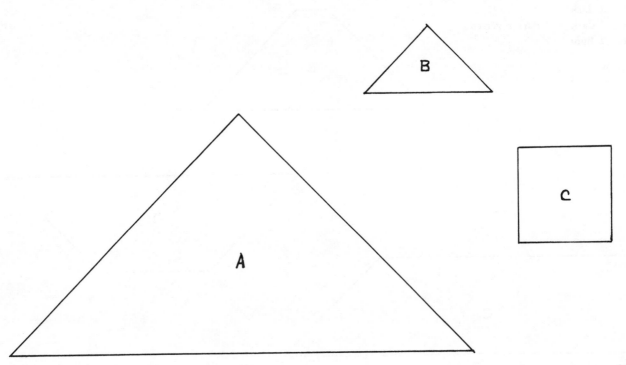

Rainbow

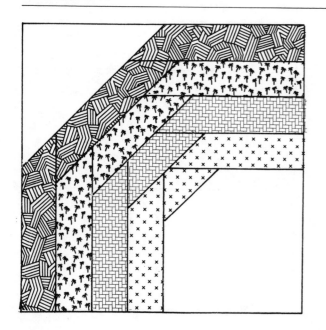

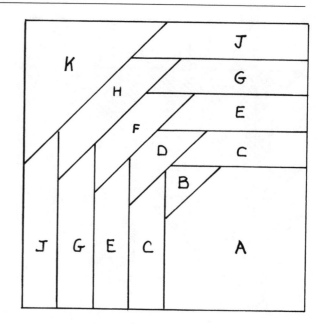

MODERATE

Pieces per block: 14

A 1 light
B 1 bright I
C 1 bright I + 1 bright I reversed
D 1 bright II
E 1 bright II + 1 bright II reversed
F 1 medium
G 1 medium + 1 medium reversed
H 1 dark
J 1 dark + 1 dark reversed
K 1 light

Children are fascinated by rainbows—the brighter the better! This design is constructed in rows around the A piece.

Sew B to the angled edge of A. Sew a C to each A-B edge. Sew D to C-B-C; sew an E to each D-C edge. Sew F to E-D-E; sew a G to each E-F edge. Sew H to G-F-G; sew a J to each G-H edge. Sew K to J-H-J to complete the design.

Outline-quilt each band of the rainbow; quilt a swirling cloud pattern across the background pieces.

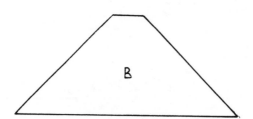

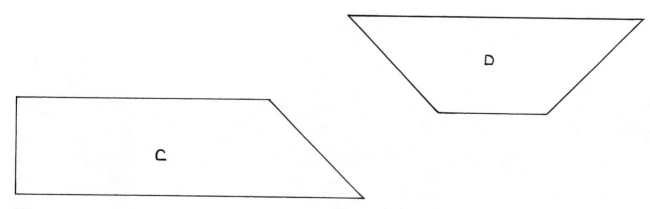

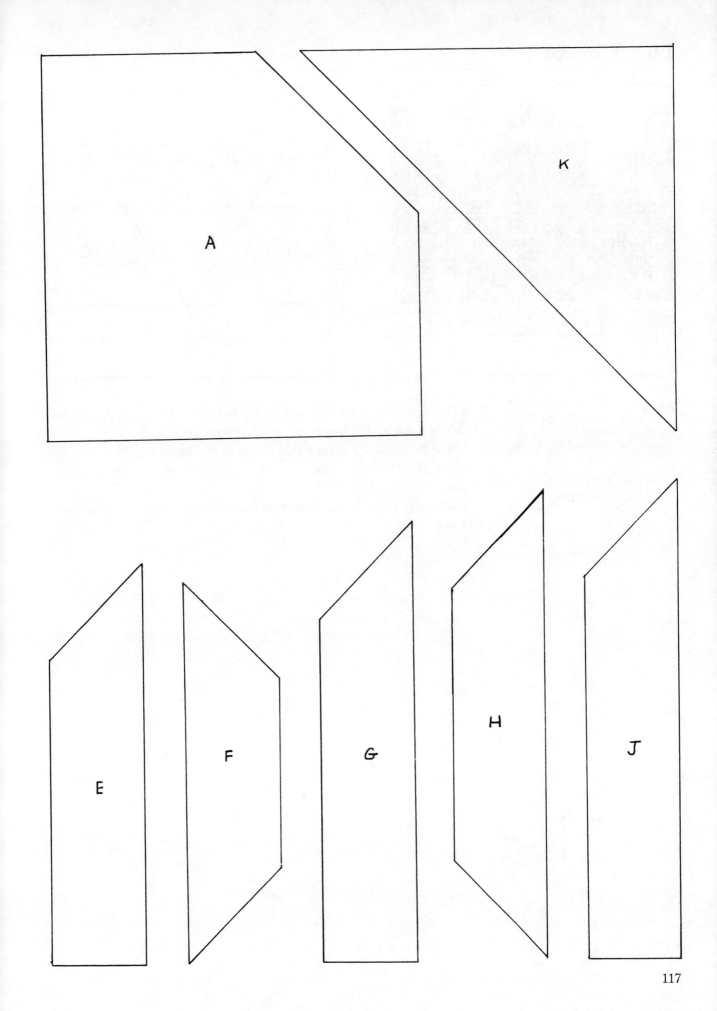

Her Majesty

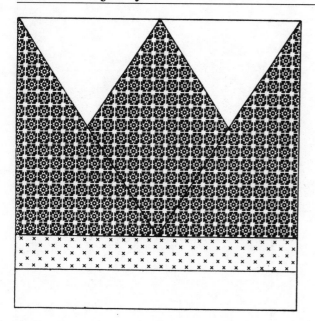

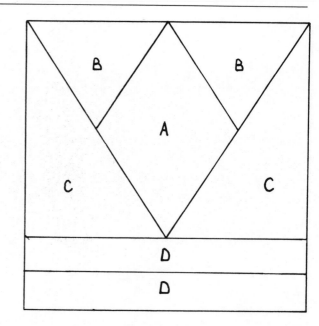

EASY

Pieces per block: 7

A   1 dark
B   2 light
C   1 dark, 1 dark reversed
D   1 light, 1 medium

An excellent addition to a quilt for the favorite little princess in your life, this block is very quick and easy to construct.

Sew a B to adjacent edges of A. Sew a C to each side of A-B. Sew the medium D to C-C. Sew the light D to the medium D to complete the design.

Outline-quilt the crown, then quilt a jewel or scroll design across the A and C pieces.

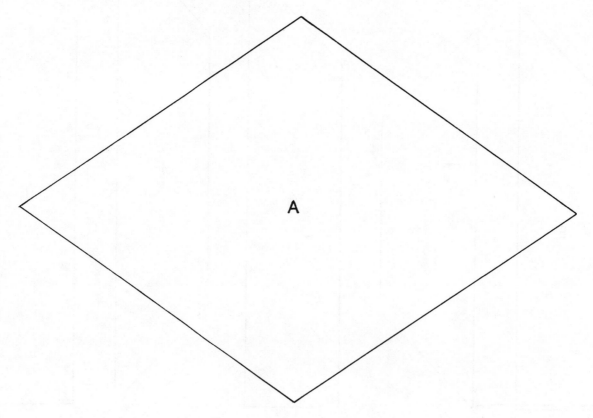

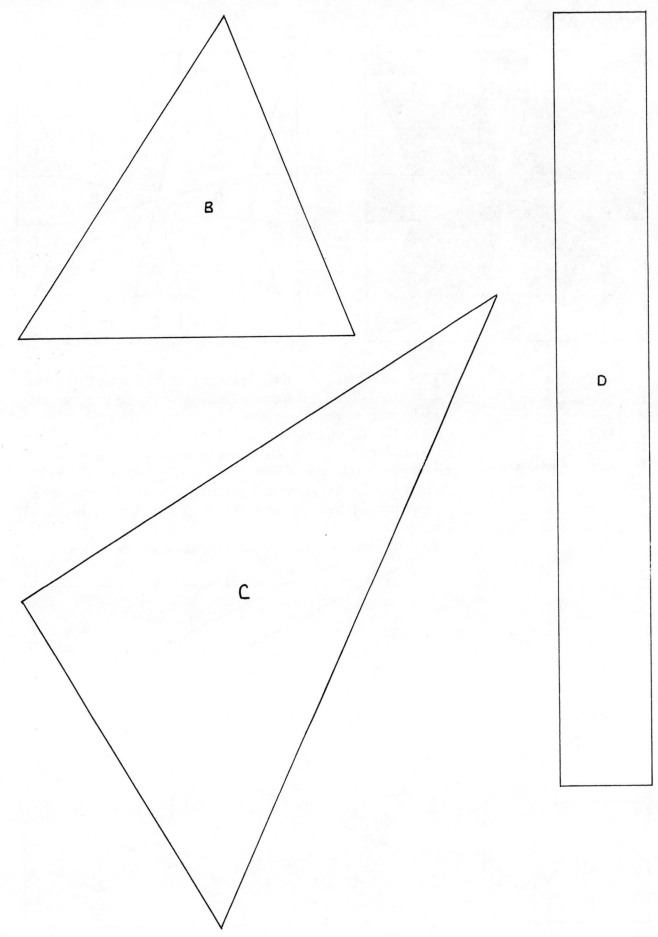

119

Sugar & Spice

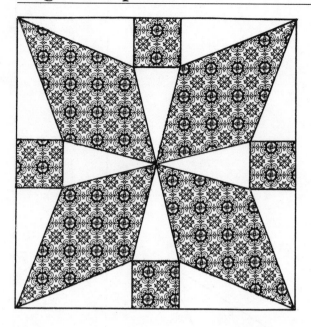

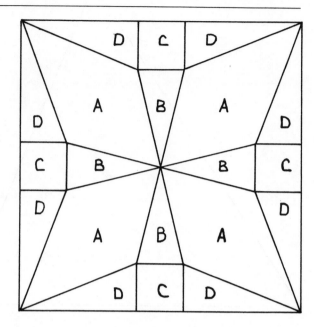

CHALLENGING

Pieces per block: 20

A   4 dark
B   4 light
C   4 dark
D   4 light + 4 light reversed

The angled seams make this design a bit difficult. To make the job easier, be sure to begin and end your stitching (at the seams that are to be angled) exactly ¼ inch from the raw edges.

Sew a B to the left edge of each A. Sew the A-B's together in 2 pairs to make each half of the central section. Sew the pairs together, matching seams carefully. Sew a D to opposite edges of each C, being sure to use reversed D's for each strip. Sew D-C-D to each open edge of the central section, angling your stitches slightly at each corner of C. Press carefully when the design is complete.

Quilt the design to emphasize the 4 diamonds and the squares.

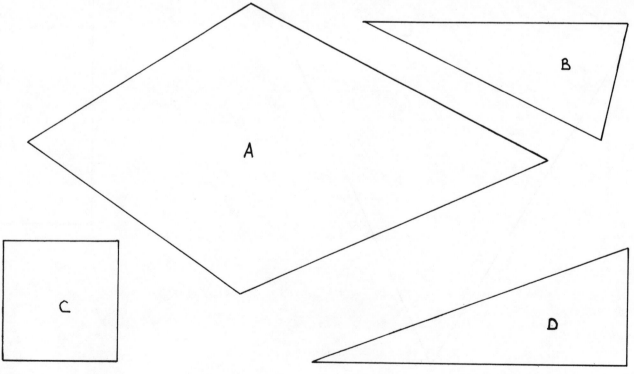

Mother Goose

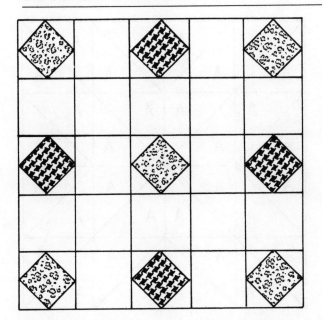

H ere's a perfect block where you can use bright scrap fabrics, making each A square a different color. The block is composed of 5 rows with 5 squares in each row.

First, assemble the A-B squares by sewing a B to each edge of A. Arrange all the squares as shown in the diagram. Sew together into strips, making 5 rows. Join the rows, matching seams carefully, to complete the design.

Outline-quilt each colored square; quilt a zigzag design across the C squares.

MODERATE

Pieces per block: 61
A   5 bright, 4 dark
B   36 light
C   16 light

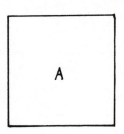

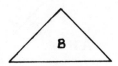

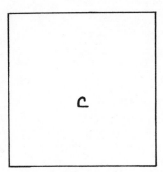

Anna's Choice Quilt

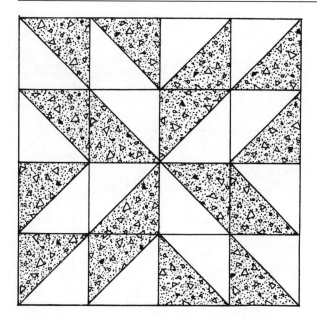
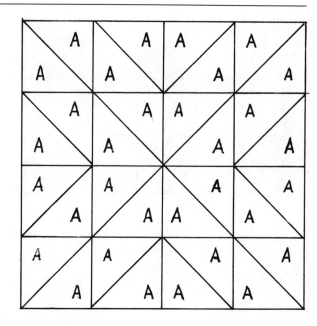

EASY

Pieces per block: 32
A   16 light, 16 dark

This pretty block is very easy to assemble. First construct all the A squares as shown in the diagram.

Arrange the A squares in 4 rows with 4 squares in each row, following the diagram for position of colors. Join the squares in rows, then sew the rows together, matching seams carefully, to complete the design.

Outline-quilt the pinwheel and the dark border triangles.

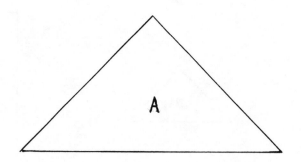

Baby Girl

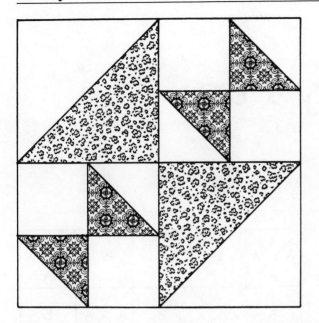
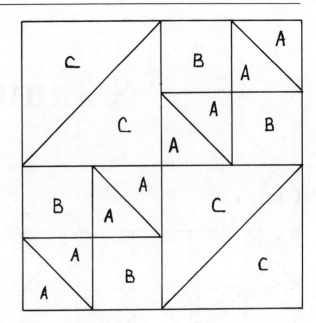

This delicate design would make a good corner block in a sampler quilt. It is composed of 4 pieced squares.

First, sew each light A to a dark A. Sew each dark A to a B. Sew 2 pairs of A-B strips together, making 2 squares. Sew each light C to a dark C, making the other 2 squares of the block. Sew 2 pairs of squares together as shown in the diagram to make each half of the block. Sew the halves together to complete the design.

Quilt along each seam of the design.

EASY

Pieces per block: 16
A 4 light, 4 dark
B 4 light
C 2 light, 2 medium

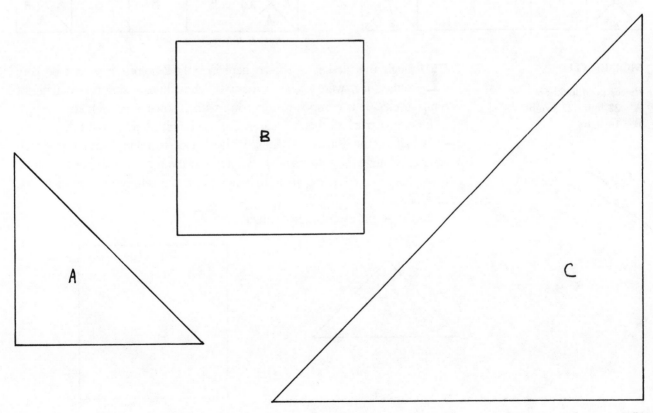

Country Fun

Clown

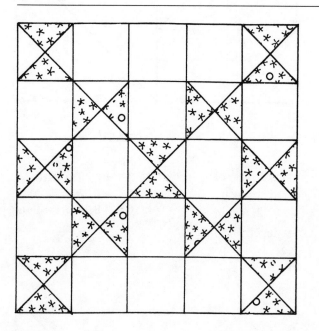

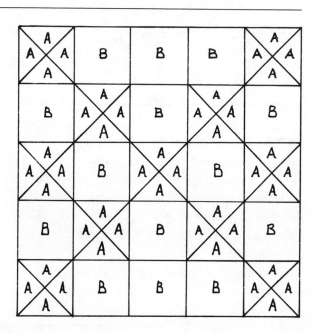

MODERATE

Pieces per block: 58

A 22 light, 22 bright

B 14 light

Though this design is shown here in only 2 colors, it would be very exciting if it were made in many different hues, using up your bright scrap fabrics. It is composed of 5 rows with 5 squares in each row.

First, construct all the A squares. Sew each light A to a bright A, making each half of the square. Then sew the halves together, completing each square. Arrange the squares as shown in the diagram; sew together, making 5 rows. Sew the rows together, matching seams carefully, to complete the design.

Outline-quilt each bright triangle.

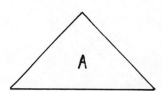

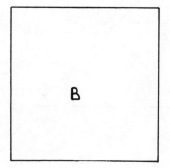

A Butterfly in Angles

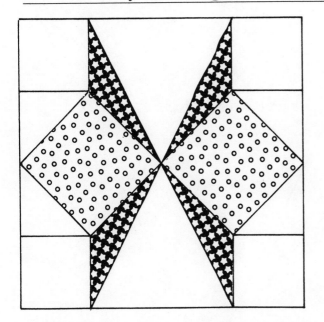

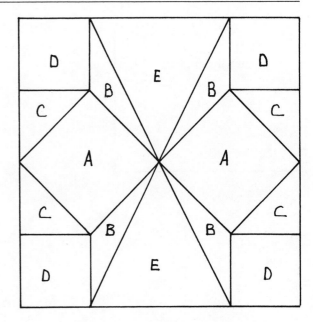

As you study the design, you'll see that it is composed of 2 halves which are joined along the diagonal formed by the B-E pieces.

Arrange all the pieces on a flat surface, then separate along the central diagonal to make assembly easier. Sew a B to adjacent sides of each A; sew a C to each remaining edge of A. Inset a D into each corner made by the B and C pieces; see How to Inset (page 15). Repeat for the opposite side. Sew an E to the upper right B of one half and the other E to the lower left B of the other half of the block. Sew the halves of the block together, matching seams carefully in the middle, to complete the design.

Outline-quilt the butterfly; quilt a cloud pattern across the background.

CHALLENGING

Pieces per block: 16
A   2 medium
B   2 dark + 2 dark reversed
C   2 light + 2 light reversed
D   4 light
E   2 light

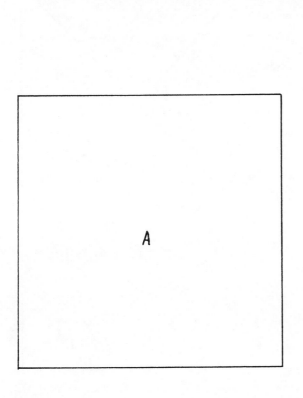

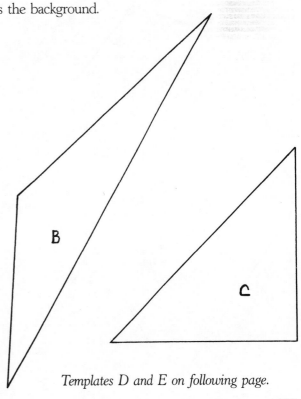

Templates D and E on following page.

125

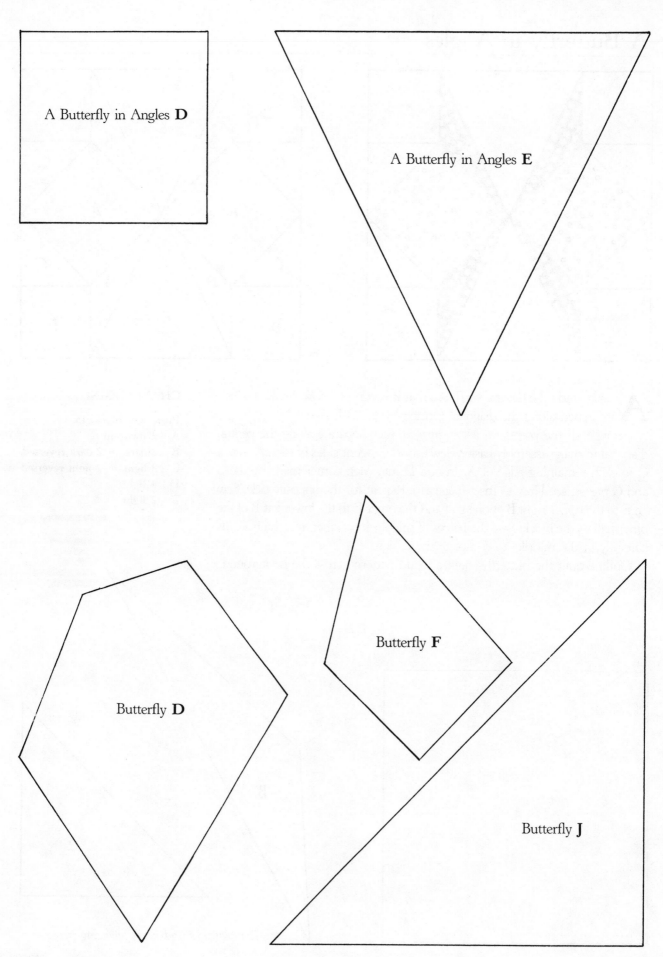

A Butterfly in Angles **D**

A Butterfly in Angles **E**

Butterfly **D**

Butterfly **F**

Butterfly **J**

Butterfly

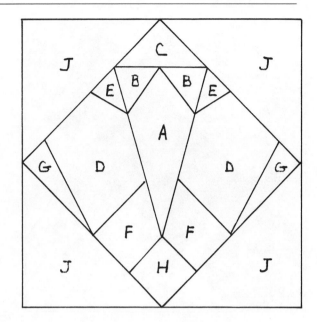

This appealing design is sure to please a cherished little girl. The central square of the block is pieced, then sewn to the 4 outer triangles.

To make the butterfly, sew a B to each short edge of A. Sew C to B-B. For each wing, sew E, F and G to D following the diagram carefully. Sew a wing to each side of the body. Inset H into the angle made by the F pieces; see How to Inset (page 15). Sew a J to each edge of the central square to complete the design.

Quilt the butterfly's wings and body; quilt a small flower in the middle of each J piece.

CHALLENGING

Pieces per block: 17
A   1 dark
B   1 light + 1 light reversed
C   1 light
D   1 bright I + 1 bright I reversed
E   1 light + 1 light reversed
F   1 bright II + 1 bright II reversed
G   1 light + 1 light reversed
H   1 light
J   4 medium

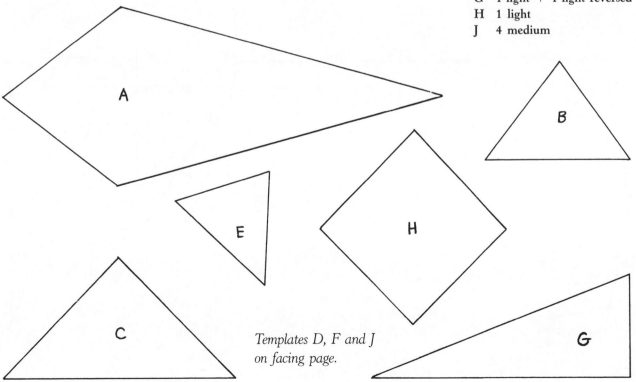

Templates D, F and J on facing page.

127

Playground

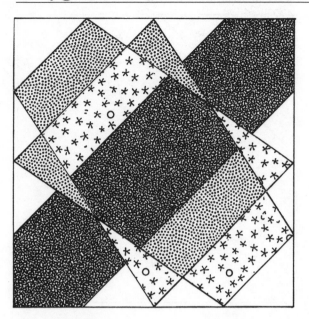

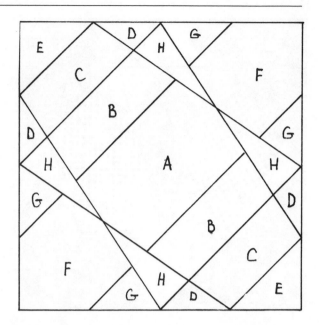

CHALLENGING

Pieces per block: 21

A   1 dark
B   1 bright, 1 medium
C   1 bright, 1 medium
D   2 light + 2 light reversed
E   2 light
F   2 dark
G   2 light + 2 light reversed
H   2 bright, 2 medium

This block is a challenge because it will take careful marking, cutting and piecing to accurately insert the G-F-G pieces into the rest of the block.

First, assemble the central diagonal strip. Sew a B to each long edge of A; sew a C to each B. Sew an E to each C. Following the diagram, sew a D to the short edge of each H. Sew D-H to each side of the diagonal strip as shown. Sew a G to each side of F. Sew G-F-G to each side of the central section, turning stitching slightly at the point of each F to complete the design. Press carefully.

Quilt along each seam of the design.

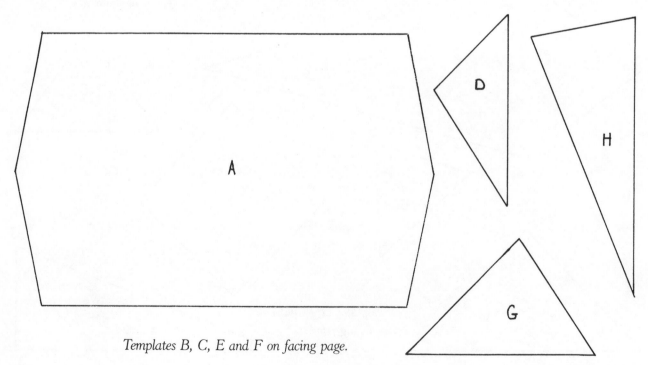

Templates B, C, E and F on facing page.

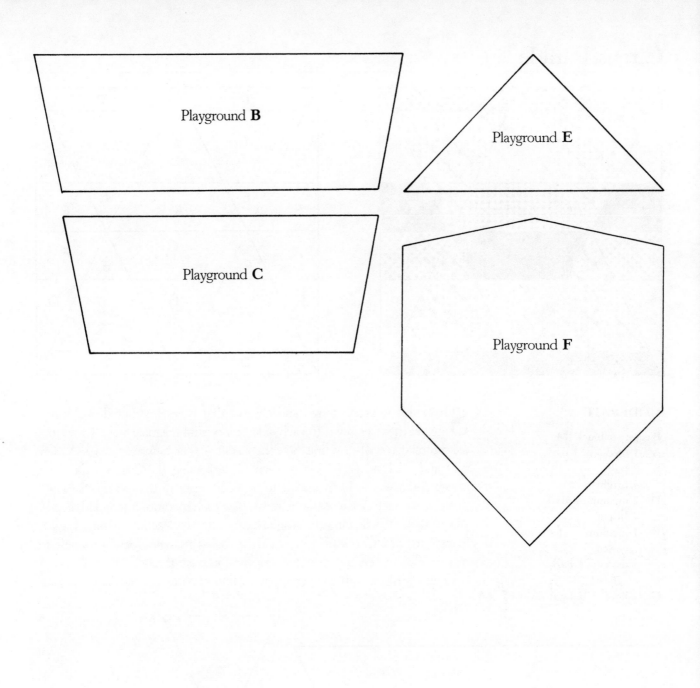

Playground **B**

Playground **E**

Playground **C**

Playground **F**

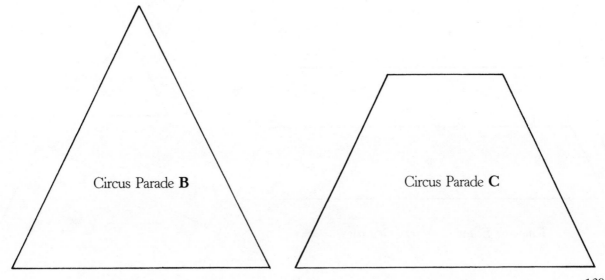

Circus Parade **B**

Circus Parade **C**

Circus Parade

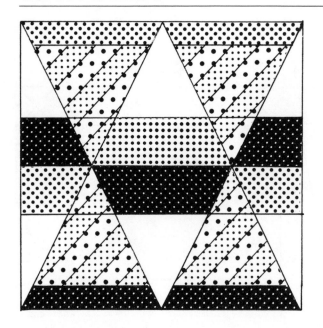
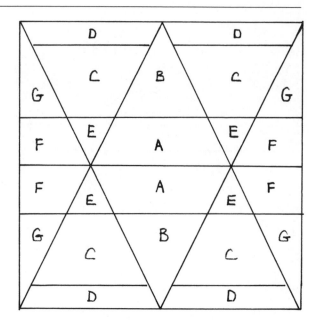

MODERATE

Pieces per block: 24

A   1 medium, 1 dark
B   2 light
C   4 bright
D   2 medium, 2 dark
E   4 bright
F   1 medium + 1 medium
    reversed,
    1 dark + 1 dark
    reversed
G   2 light + 2 light reversed

S tudy this unusual design and observe that it is constructed of 2 right-angled triangles sewn to each side of a central diagonal strip. Construct the central diagonal strip first. Sew the 2 A's together. Sew a B to each A. Sew a D and an E to each side of each C. Following the diagram for color placement, sew a C-D-E triangle to opposite edges of the central diamond.

Next, construct each of the triangles. Sew each medium F to a dark F; sew a G to each F. Following the diagram carefully, sew each remaining C-D-E triangle to each G-F strip to form right-angled triangles. Sew a triangle to each side of the central diagonal strip to complete the design.

Quilt the block with an overlapping diamond pattern, ignoring the seams.

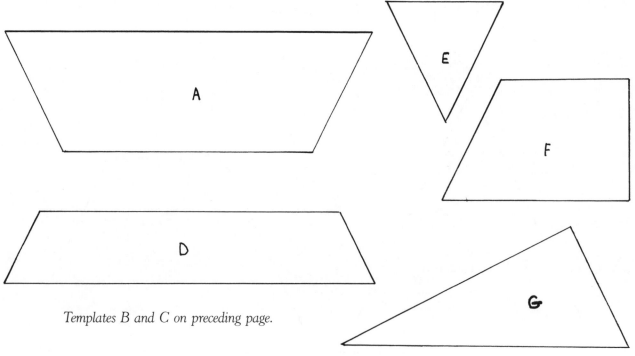

Templates B and C on preceding page.

Farmer's Daughter

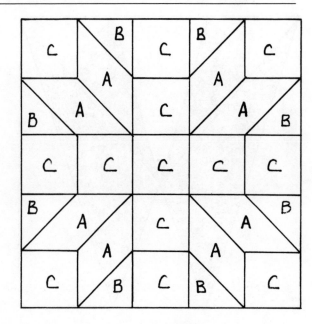

Insetting is required at each corner of this striking design; see How to Inset (page 15). The block is composed of 4 pieced squares joined by the central C strips.

To make each square, sew reversed A's together; sew a B to each A. Inset a bright C into the angle formed by the A's. Following the diagram, sew a bright C to each medium C to make 4 C strips. Join 2 sets of pieced A-B-C squares by sewing one to each side of a C strip. Sew the bright squares of the remaining 2 C strips to each side of the remaining medium C. Sew the top and bottom sections to each side of the C strip just made to complete the design.

Quilt close to each seam of the design, including the outer border.

CHALLENGING

Pieces per block: 29
A   4 light + 4 light reversed
B   8 dark
C   8 bright, 5 medium

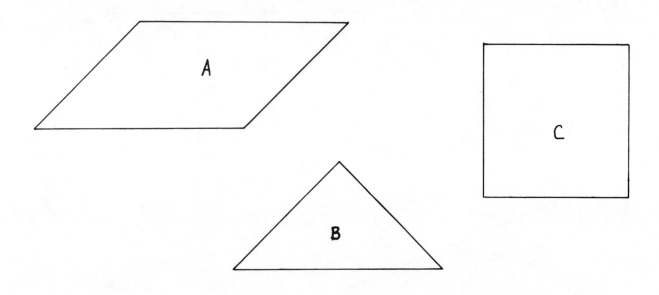

Swallowtail Butterfly

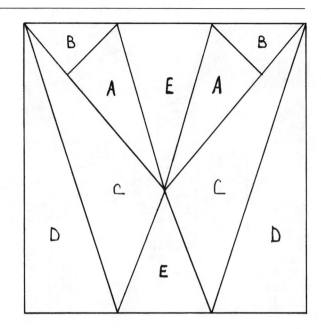

MODERATE

Pieces per block: 10

A 1 medium + 1 medium reversed
B 1 light + 1 light reversed
C 1 bright + 1 bright reversed
D 1 light + 1 light reversed
E 2 light

A graceful design, this block is constructed in 2 halves along the diagonal formed by the A, C and E pieces.

Sew A to B as shown in the diagram. Sew A-B to C. Sew C to D. Sew an E to the A of the top half and to the C of the bottom half of the block to make the central diagonal. Sew the halves together, matching seams carefully in the middle, to complete the design.

Outline-quilt the butterfly; quilt a swirling cloud pattern across the background.

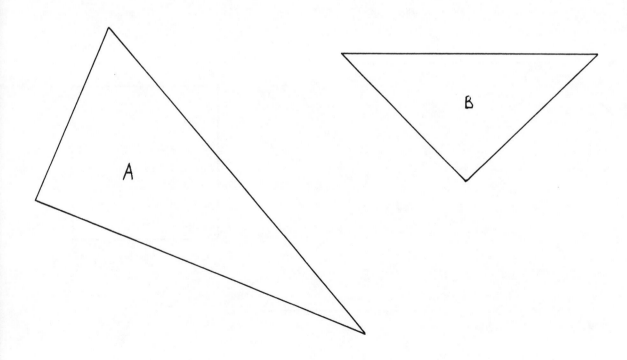

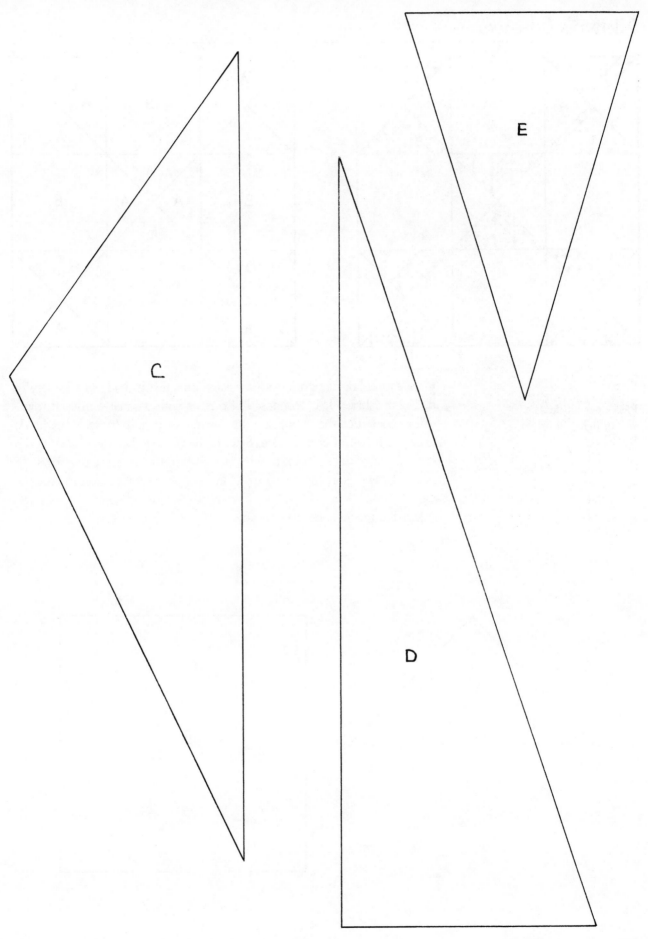

C

D

E

Clown's Choice

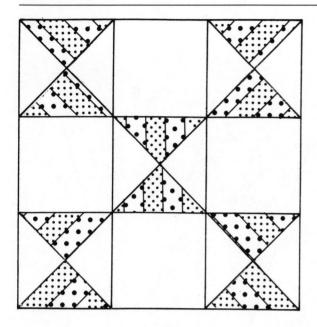

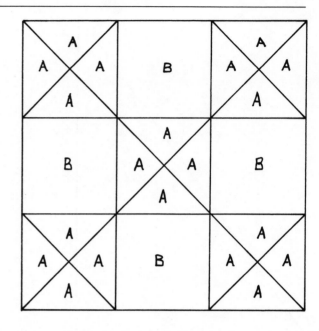

EASY

Pieces per block: 24
A   10 light, 10 bright
B   4 light

This appealing design looks especially attractive if made in a variety of bright fabrics. It is composed of 3 rows with 3 squares in each row.

First, construct the A squares by sewing each light A to a bright A, making each half of each square. Sew the halves together to complete each square. Arrange the A and B squares as shown in the diagram; sew together, making 3 rows. Join the rows, matching seams carefully, to complete the design.

Quilt the block along every seam.

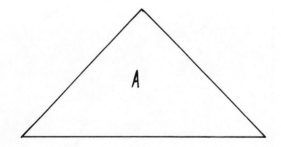

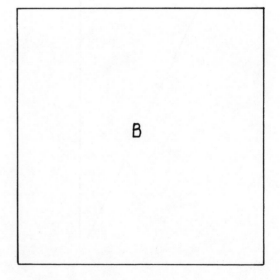

Toys & Games

Tick-Tack-Toe

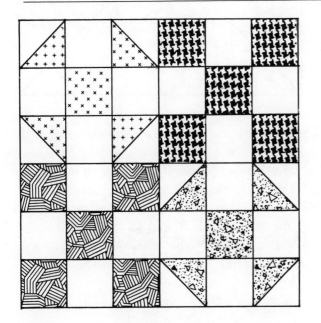

This simple design is easily constructed in horizontal rows. Construct all the A squares first by sewing a white A to each of the patterned A's. Arrange the A and B squares as shown in the diagram; assemble in 6 horizontal rows. Sew the rows together, matching seams carefully, to complete the design.

Outline-quilt each patterned piece of the design but not the white ones.

EASY

Pieces per block: 44

A   8 white, 4 light,
     4 medium
B   16 white, 1 light,
     5 bright, 1 medium, 5
dark

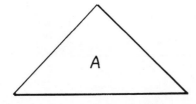

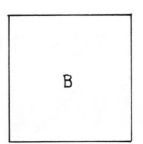

Blind Man's Buff

(Color photo, page A1)

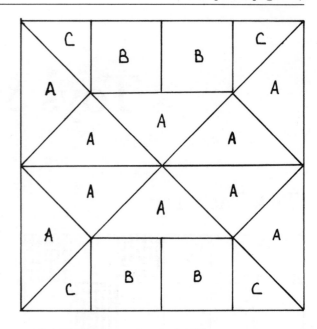

EASY

Pieces per block: 18

A 2 light, 2 bright I,
    2 bright II, 2 medium,
    2 dark
B 2 light, 2 dark
C 4 medium

Study the diagram. You'll see that the block is composed of 4 pieced triangles.

Following the diagram, assemble each of the 2 side triangles by sewing together 4 A triangles. To assemble the top and bottom triangles, sew together the light and dark B squares; sew a C on each side of each B strip. Sew a medium A to the long edge of each B strip to create the pattern indicated in the diagram. Sew the triangles together in the order shown in the diagram to form the 2 halves. Sew the halves together, matching seams carefully, to complete the block.

Outline-quilt the design, then quilt a zigzag pattern across the B pieces.

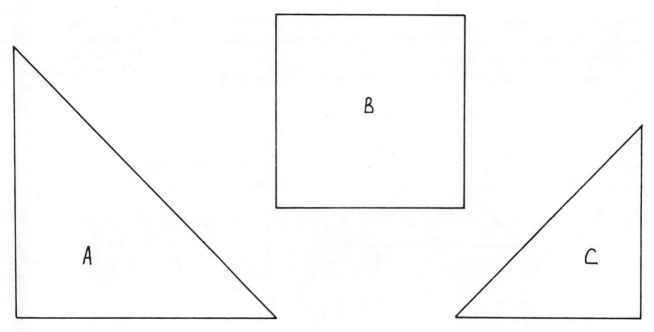

Building Blocks

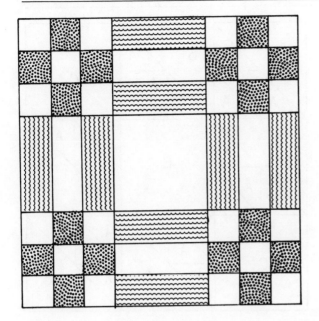

A	A	A	B	A	A	A
A	A	A	B	A	A	A
A	A	A	B	A	A	A
B	B	B	C	B	B	B
A	A	A	B	A	A	A
A	A	A	B	A	A	A
A	A	A	B	A	A	A

Beginners who need practice in matching seams would do well to try this block; accurate cutting and sewing are essential.

Assemble the 4 corner blocks first by sewing together alternately the light and dark A pieces; first, sew the blocks in horizontal rows, then sew the rows together, matching seams carefully. Next, assemble the B squares by sewing a dark B to each side of a light B. Join the blocks in 3 horizontal rows as shown in the diagram; then join the rows, matching seams carefully, to complete the design.

Starting with the central square, quilt the block to form concentric squares.

EASY

Pieces per block: 49
A   20 light, 16 dark
B   4 light, 8 medium
C   1 light

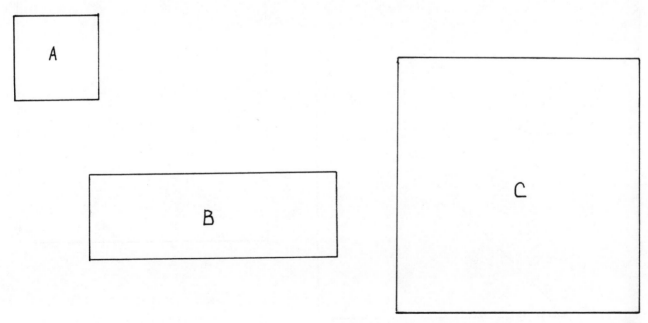

Cat's Cradle

(Color photos, pages A1 and H2)

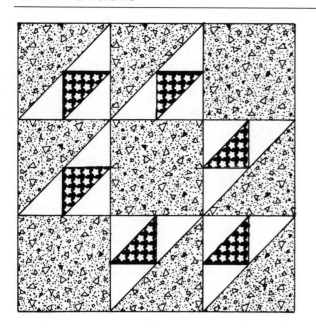

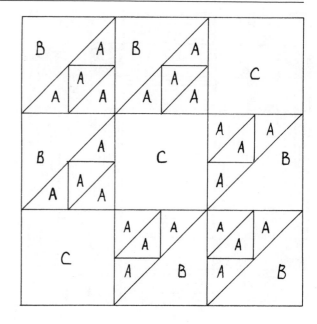

EASY

Pieces per block: 33
A 18 light, 6 dark
B 6 medium
C 3 medium

Simple yet elegant, this design becomes a dramatic focal point in any sampler quilt; it is composed of 9 squares.

First, assemble the pieced squares. Sew the A's together as shown in the diagram, forming 6 triangles. Sew each A triangle to a B, creating a square. Join the A-B squares to the C's and each other in 3 horizontal rows, following the diagram. Sew the rows together, matching seams carefully, to complete the design.

Quilt around the edges of each large A triangle and the central triangles, then quilt the outer edge of the block.

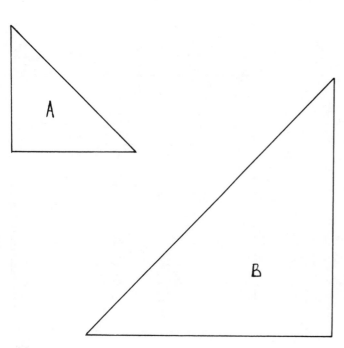

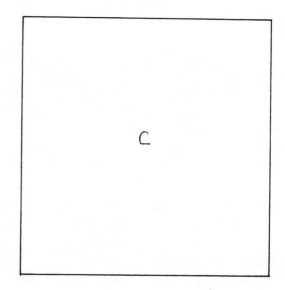

Charades

(Color photo, page A1)

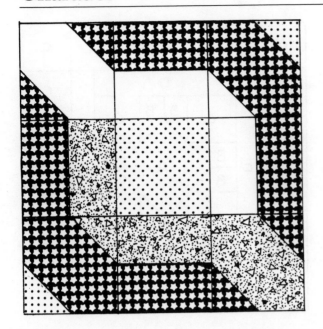
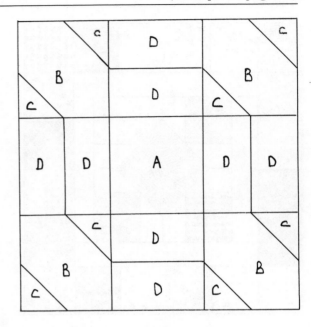

Though it creates the illusion of a diagonal design, this block is actually sewn together in squares, then in horizontal rows.

Construct the B-C squares first, carefully following the diagram, to arrange color combinations. Next, assemble the D squares as shown. Arrange all the squares following the diagram; join the squares in 3 horizontal rows. Sew the rows together, matching seams carefully, to complete the design.

Continue the diagonal "charade" by quilting around the central area to emphasize the diagonal effect.

EASY

Pieces per block: 21
A   1 bright
B   1 light, 1 medium, 2 dark
C   1 light, 2 bright, 1 medium, 4 dark
D   2 light, 2 medium, 4 dark

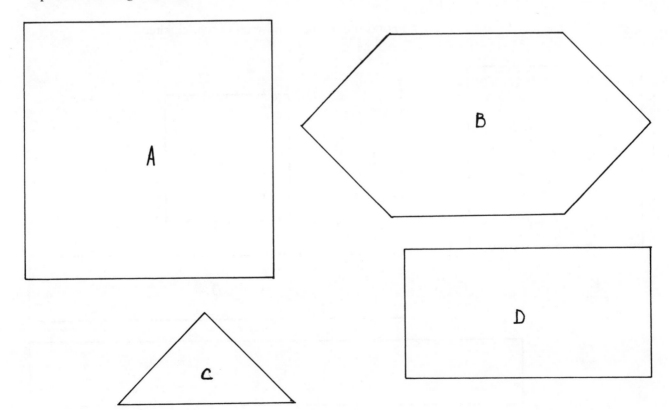

139

Farmer in the Dell

(Color photo, page A1)

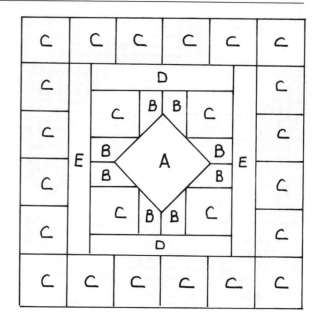

MODERATE

Pieces per block: 37

A	1 medium
B	4 light + 4 light reversed
C	24 assorted
D	2 light
E	2 light

The "farmer" is the central square of the block. He is surrounded by the various "children" playing the game. Use all your scraps to make this block as bright and interesting as possible.

To begin, sew a B to each side of a C. Sew a B-C-B to each edge of A, then sew together the remaining edges of the B's. Sew a D to the top and bottom and an E to each side of the central square. Sew the C's together in 2 groups of 4 squares and 2 groups of 6 squares. Sew the 4-square strips to each side of the central section. Sew the remaining strips to the top and bottom.

Quilt around the "farmer" and each of the "children."

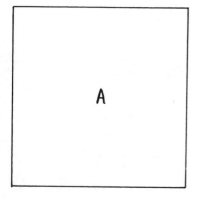

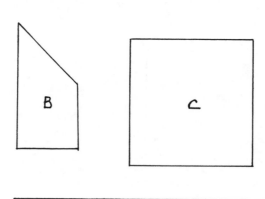

Follow the Leader

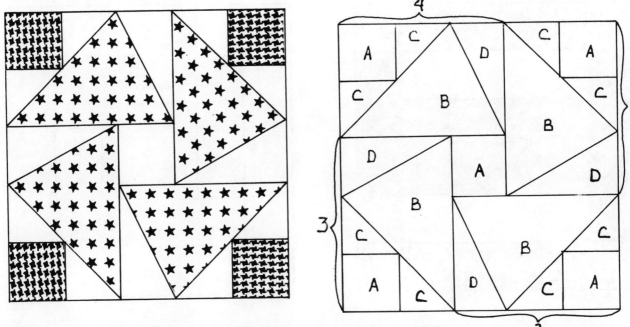

To create this clean and simple design, 4 rectangles are pieced together, then sewn in a clockwise manner around the central square.

To begin, sew a C to each side of the 4 dark A's as shown in the diagram. Sew C-C to B. Sew D to B to complete the rectangle.

To assemble the block, begin in the upper right corner with rectangle 1; sew this rectangle to A. Next sew rectangle 2 to A and to rectangle 1. Then sew rectangle 3 to A and to rectangle 2. Finally, sew rectangle 4 to rectangle 3 and A, turning stitching sharply to continue sewing 4 to 1.

Quilt around each large triangle and each corner square; quilt a second line of stitches ½ inch from the first, inside the triangles and squares.

MODERATE

Pieces per block: 21

A	1 light, 4 dark
B	4 medium
C	8 light
D	4 light

Guessing Game

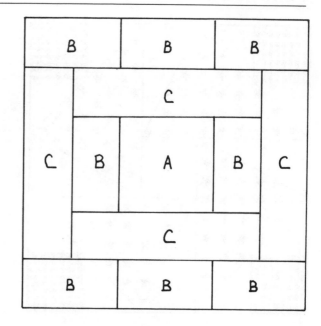

EASY

Pieces per block: 13

A 1 dark

B 2 light I, 4 medium,
      2 dark

C 2 light II, 2 dark

Depending upon how you arrange your colors, children will have fun guessing what this design really represents!

Sew a light B to each side of A. Sew a light C to the top and bottom of B-A-B. Sew a dark C to each side of C-B-C. Construct the top and bottom B strips by sewing a medium B to each side of a dark B. Sew to the top and bottom of the block.

Quilt the design to emphasize the dark central strip and the circular effect of the middle B and C strips.

A

B

C

Hide & Seek

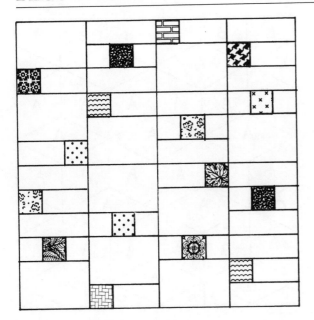

This block is not only fun to make, but children also will love the bright spots of color. Use up your scrap fabrics to make the design bright and cheery.

If you study the diagram, you'll notice that the block is actually made up of 16 squares, each composed of 3 to 5 pieces.

Assemble all of the squares first, following the diagram. Arrange the pieced squares as shown in the diagram; sew together in 4 horizontal rows, matching seams carefully. Sew the rows together to complete the design.

Quilt around each colored square and around the edge of the block.

EASY

Pieces per block: 61
A 10 light
B 14 light, 16 assorted
C 12 light
D 9 light

Blocks

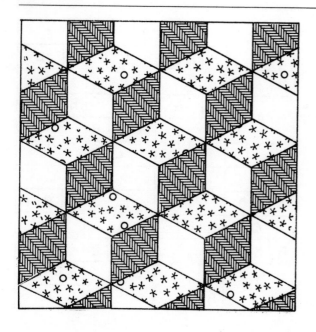

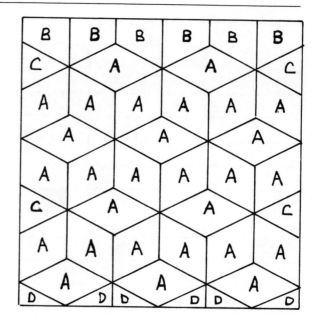

CHALLENGING

Pieces per block: 44

A 9 light, 10 medium, 9 dark

B 3 light, 3 dark reversed

C 4 medium

D 3 light, 3 dark reversed

A wonderful optical illusion is achieved by the rhythmic juxtaposition of the varied diamond-shaped A pieces. Be very accurate when cutting and piecing; see How to Inset (page 15).

Sew each light A to a dark A, forming 3 zigzag horizontal rows. Inset a medium A into each angle formed by the light and dark A's. Sew the rows together in the same manner. Sew the C's at the left and right ends of the first and third rows. Inset the remaining A's along the bottom of the A section as shown in the diagram.

For the top row, sew each light B to a dark B. Inset this row into the top of the A section. For the bottom row, sew 2 pairs of dark and light D's together. Inset into the bottom of the block. Sew the remaining D's to the corners.

Outline-quilt each edge of the blocks.

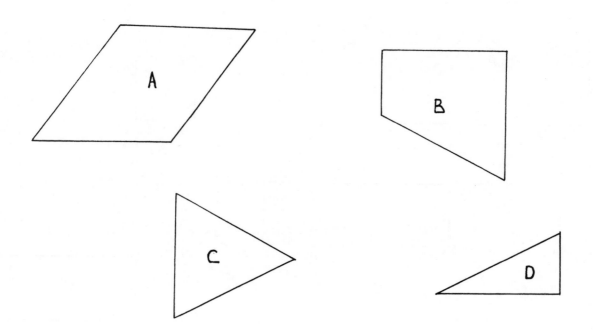

Seesaw

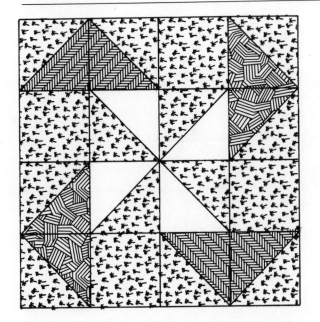

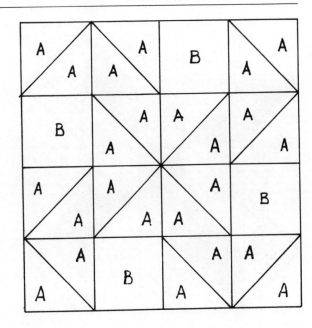

A wonderful feeling of motion is achieved by the coloring of the A triangles. The design is composed of 4 rows with 4 squares in each row.

Construct all the A squares first by sewing a medium A to a light or dark A. Arrange the pieces as shown in the diagram. Join the squares in 4 rows. Then join the rows, matching seams carefully, to complete the design.

Quilt the block to emphasize the "seesaw" effect.

EASY

Pieces per block: 28
A 4 light, 12 medium,
     4 dark I, 4 dark II
B 4 medium

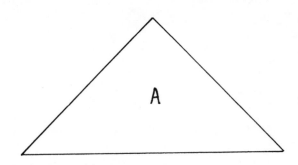

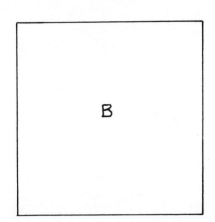

Jack-in-the-Box

(Color photo, page A1)

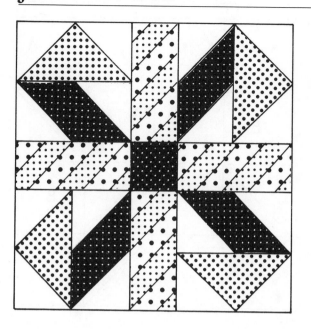

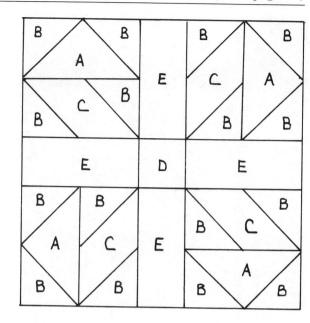

EASY

Pieces per block: 29

A	4	bright
B	16	light
C	4	dark
D	1	dark
E	4	medium

An exciting feeling of motion is created by the placement of the A and C pieces.

Sew the 4 corner squares first. Sew a B to adjacent sides of A, then sew a B to opposite sides of C following the diagram. Sew A to B-C-B to complete each square. Arrange the squares and the remaining pieces as shown in the diagram. Join the top squares by sewing one to each side of an E strip. Repeat for the bottom squares. Sew an E to each side of the D. Sew the top and bottom to each side of E-D-E to complete the design.

Quilt around the A, C and E pieces.

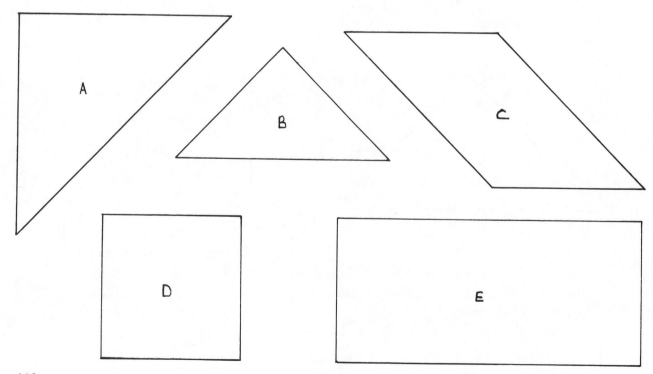

Red Light/Green Light

(Color photos, pages A1 and H3)

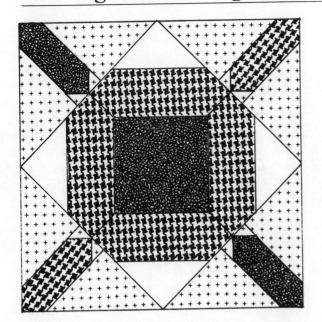

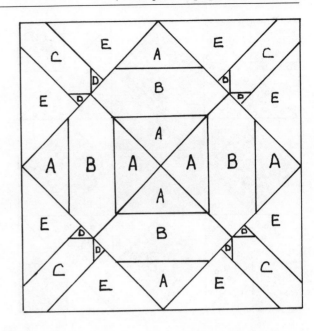

Study the block carefully; you'll notice that it is composed of 4 pieced (A-B-A) squares and 4 pieced (C-D-E) triangles. The D pieces are a bit tricky because they're so small, but the finished effect is worth the effort.

Construct the squares by sewing a light and dark A to each side of each B. Assemble the triangles by sewing 2 D's to an end of each C; sew an E to each side of D-C. To complete the block, join the 4 squares to form the middle; then sew a triangle to each corner.

Quilt around each bright, medium and dark piece.

CHALLENGING

Pieces per block: 32

A   4 light, 4 dark
B   4 medium
C   2 medium, 2 dark
D   8 bright
E   8 bright

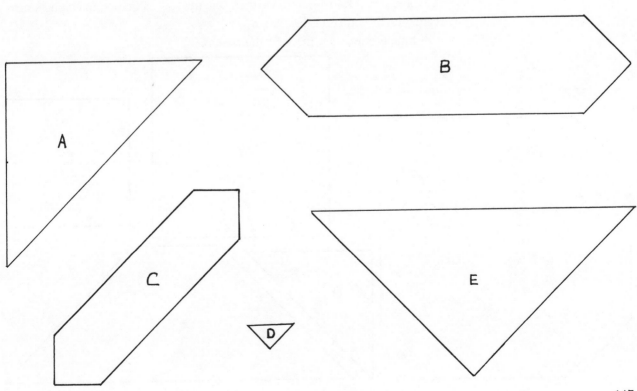

Kaleidoscope

(Color photos, pages A1 and H4)

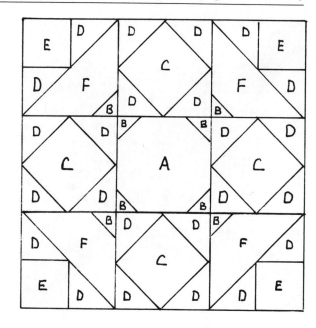

MODERATE

Pieces per block: 45

A   1 dark I
B   8 medium I
C   4 dark II
D   16 light I, 8 light II
E   4 medium II
F   4 bright

This design can produce a variety of effects depending on your placement of the bright and dark fabrics. If you want to accentuate the star shape in the middle, make the central D's in a bright rather than light fabric.

Study the block; you'll notice that it is composed of 9 pieced squares. Begin constructing the central square by sewing a B to each short edge of A. Next, construct each of the 4 side squares by sewing a D to each edge of C. Finally, construct each corner square by sewing a B to the short edge of F; sew a D to adjacent edges of E. Then sew the long edge of the triangle thus made to the long edge of F. Arrange the blocks as shown in the diagram. Join the blocks in 3 horizontal rows, then sew the rows together, matching seams carefully, to complete the design.

Outline-quilt each piece of the design.

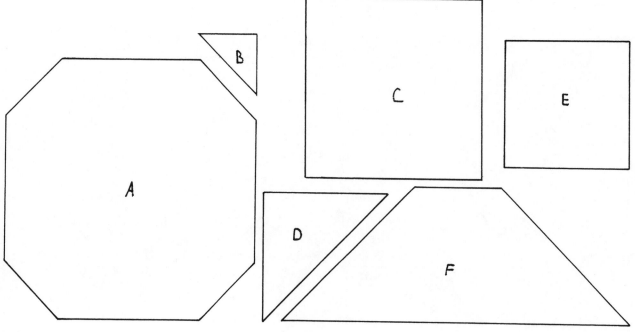

Tag

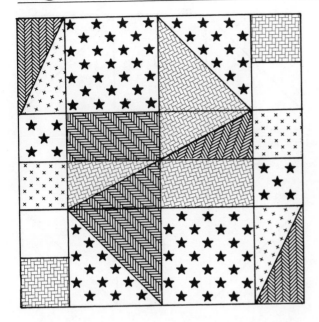
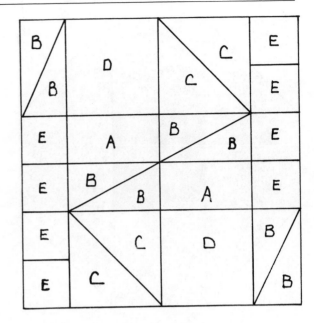

This frivolous design imitates the aimless directions taken by children playing tag. Although it is easy sewing, there are many seams to match, so careful cutting and piecing are essential.

The block is composed of 4 horizontal strips. Construct the 2 central strips first. Sew the light and dark B's together to form 2 rectangles. Sew an A to each B rectangle following the diagram. Sew an E to the ends of each A-B strip. Sew the 2 central strips together, matching seams carefully.

Construct the upper and lower strips next. Construct 2 C squares following the diagram. Sew a D to each of the C squares. Make 2 B rectangles following the diagram. Sew 2 pairs of E's together, forming 2 rectangles. Following the diagram for placement, sew a B to D, D to C-C and C-C to E-E to complete each strip. Sew the upper and lower strips to the central strip to complete the design.

Outline-quilt each piece in the block.

MODERATE

Pieces per block: 24

A 1 medium, 1 dark

B 2 light reversed,
   2 medium,
   2 dark + 2 dark reversed

C 2 bright, 1 medium,
   1 dark

D 2 bright

E 2 white, 2 light,
   2 bright, 2 medium

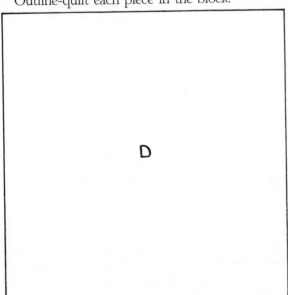
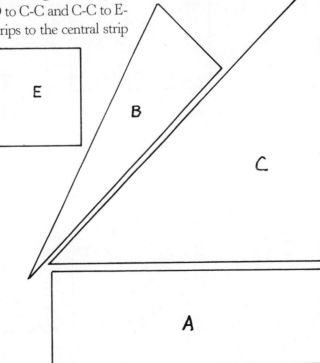

149

Ring-Around-a-Rosy

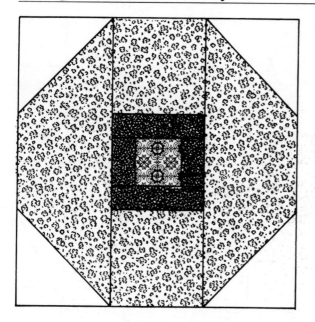
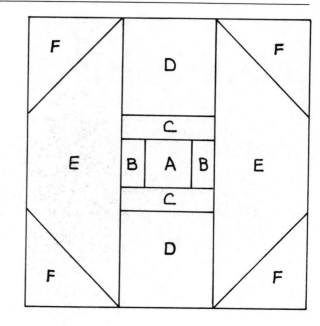

EASY

Pieces per block: 13

A	1 medium
B	2 dark
C	2 dark
D	2 bright
E	2 bright
F	4 light

This very simple block looks striking in shades of bright pink and red. Sew a B to opposite sides of A. Sew a C to each side of B-A-B. Sew a D to each C. Sew an E to each side of the pieced strip. Sew an F to each angled edge of E to complete the design.

Quilt the block in concentric rings.

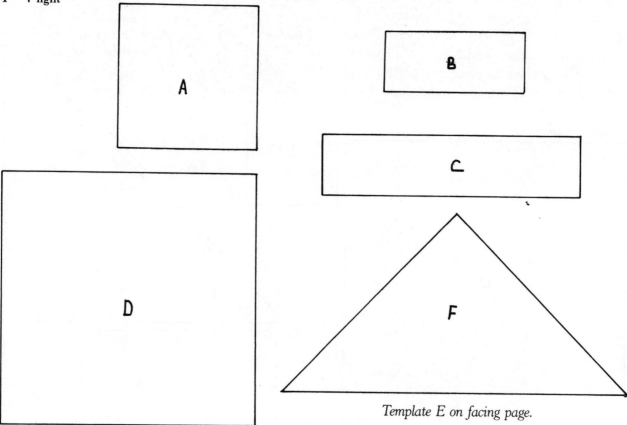

Template E on facing page.

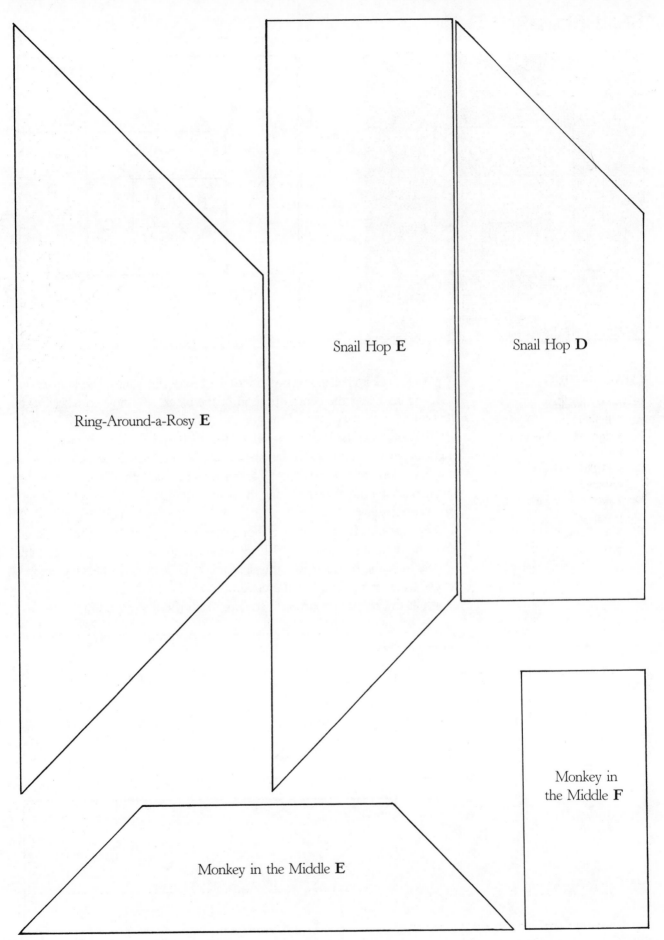

Ring-Around-a-Rosy **E**

Snail Hop **E**

Snail Hop **D**

Monkey in the Middle **F**

Monkey in the Middle **E**

Snail Hop

(Color photo, page A1)

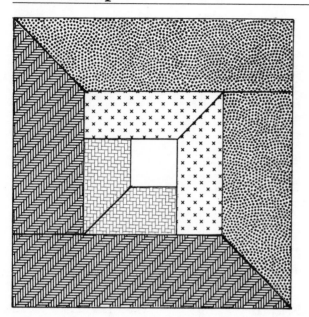

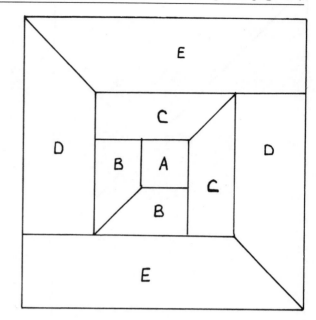

CHALLENGING

Pieces per block: 9

A 1 light I
B 1 light II + 1 light II
  reversed
C 1 bright + 1 bright
  reversed
D 1 medium, 1 dark
  reversed
E 1 medium, 1 dark
  reversed

This block is challenging because each of the 4 right-angled sections must be inset into the central portion of the block. See How to Inset (page 15).

To begin, sew the B's together along the angled edges; inset the A into the right angle made by the B's as shown in the diagram. Next, sew the C's together along the angled edges; inset the other corner of the A into the right angle made by the C's, continuing the seam to join A-B to C. This completes the central square.

Sew medium D to medium E along the straight edges. Inset the C corner into the right angle made by D-E. Sew dark D to dark E along the straight edges. Inset the B corner into the right angle made by D-E. Sew the angled edges together to complete the design.

Quilt the block in concentric squares, each about ½ inch apart.

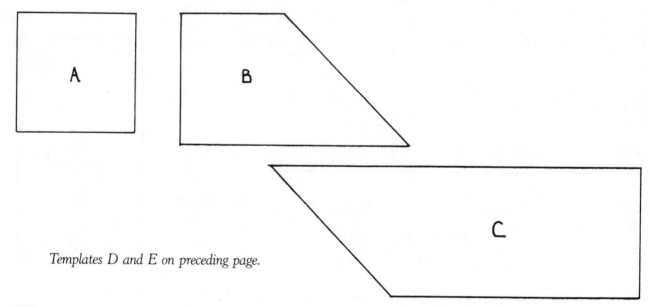

Templates D and E on preceding page.

Monkey in the Middle

(Color photo, page A1)

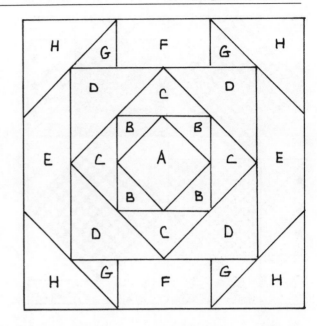

MODERATE

Pieces per block: 25

A	1	dark I
B	4	medium
C	4	dark II
D	4	bright
E	2	light
F	2	medium
G	4	light
H	4	medium

An illusion of depth can be created with an effective combination of colors and prints. This design is constructed by a series of widening squares and diamonds beginning with a central diamond.

To begin, sew a B to each edge of A; sew a C to each long edge thus created. Sew a D to each corner, forming a large square. Sew an E to each side of the square. Sew a G to each short edge of F. Sew G-F-G to each D-D edge. Sew an H to each corner to complete the design.

Quilt the block to emphasize each concentric square and the angled background (E-G) strip.

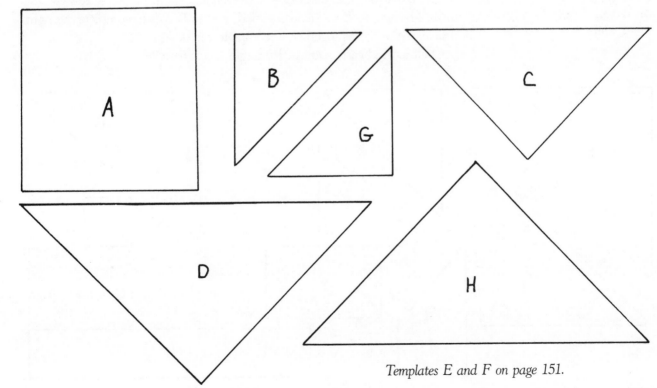

Templates E and F on page 151.

153

Tiddlywinks

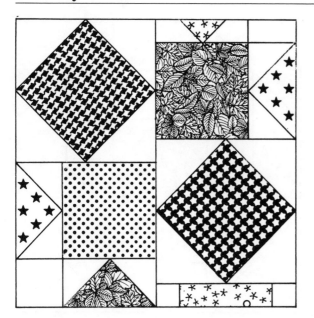

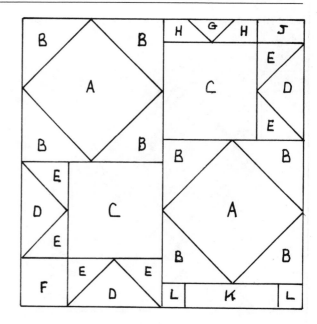

MODERATE

Pieces per block: 29

A	1 dark I, 1 dark II
B	8 white
C	1 medium I, 1 medium II
D	2 bright, 1 medium II
E	6 white
F	1 white
G	1 light
H	2 white
J	1 white
K	1 light
L	2 white

Use up your fabric scraps for this block—the more colors the better! Study the design; you'll see that the block is made up in left and right halves, with squares and rectangles in each half.

Construct the A-B squares first by sewing a B to each edge of A. Next, following the diagram for color placement, sew E to the shorter edges of each D to make 3 E-D-E pieces. Sew an E-E to a side of each C. For the left half, sew an F to the third E-D-E as shown; sew to the C-D-E piece. Sew the square just made to an A-B square to complete the left half.

For the right half, sew an H to each side of G; sew J to H as shown in the diagram. Sew the strip just made to the remaining C-D-E piece. Sew C-D-E to B-A-B. Sew an L to each edge of K; sew to B-A-B to complete the right half. Sew the halves together to complete the design.

Quilt around each patterned triangle and square.

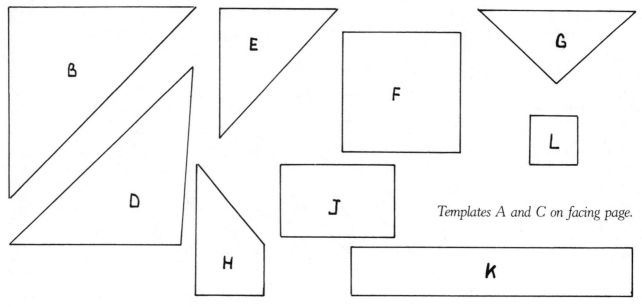

Templates A and C on facing page.

Tiddlywinks **A**

Tiddlywinks **C**

Simon Says **A**

Simon Says **G**

Simon Says

(Color photo, page A1)

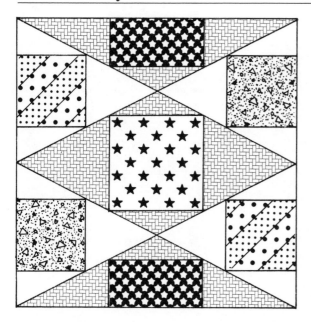

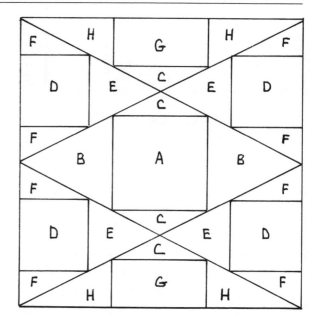

MODERATE

Pieces per block: 29

A   1 bright

B   2 light II

C   4 light II

D   2 medium I, 2 medium II

E   4 light I

F   4 light I + 4 light I reversed

G   2 dark

H   2 light II + 2 light II reversed

It is important to accurately mark and cut the pieces for this block to ensure perfect corners of the squares and triangles. Study the block; you'll see that it is composed of 2 right-angled triangles (upper right and lower left) connected by a parallelogram that extends diagonally across the middle.

To begin, construct the parallelogram. Sew a B to opposite sides of A; sew a C to the remaining edges of A. Construct the D-E-F triangles next: sew an E to one edge of D; sew an F to the adjacent upper and lower edges of D. Sew the D-E-F triangles to each edge of the middle as shown in the diagram.

Next, construct the right triangles. Make 2 D-E-F triangles as described above. Sew a C to one long edge of each G. Sew an H to each short edge of G. Sew a D-E-F triangle to a C-G-H triangle. Matching seams carefully, sew a right triangle to each side of the central parallelogram to complete the design.

Quilt the block to emphasize the squares and rectangles.

Templates A and G on preceding page.

156

This Little Piggy

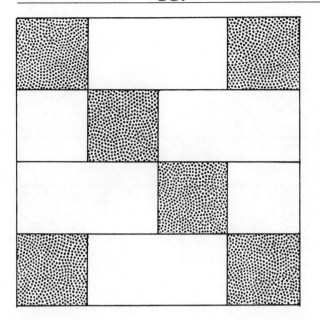

A	B	A
A	A	B
B	A	A
A	B	A

Novice quilters will enjoy making this block because it is so quick and easy to construct. A striking crib quilt could be made using only this design by constructing 4 identical blocks. Join the blocks without stripping, turning the blocks so the design forms an **X** across the middle; see the quilt requirements of the 4-Block Quilt (page 24) for fabric amounts and measurements.

Construct the block in 4 horizontal rows. To assemble each row, sew the A's and B's together following the diagram. Join the rows, matching seams carefully where necessary, to complete the design.

Outline-quilt all the dark squares.

EASY

Pieces per block: 12
A 2 light, 6 dark
B 4 light

A	B

Leapfrog

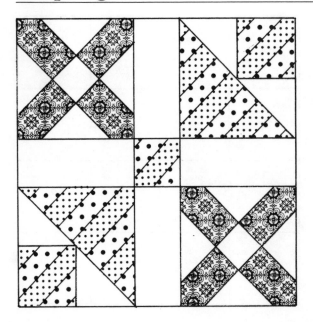
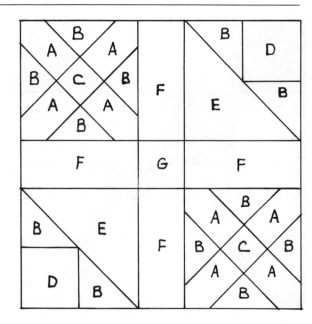

EASY

Pieces per block: 31

A	8	dark
B	12	light
C	2	light
D	2	medium
E	2	medium
F	4	light
G	1	medium

This block is very quick and easy to sew and looks excellent in a variety of color schemes.

Begin by constructing the upper left and lower right squares; sew a B to each side of 4 A's, making 4 triangles. Sew the short edges of the remaining A's to each side of a C. Sew the B-A-B's to each side of the A-C-A's to complete the squares. Next, construct the upper right and lower left squares; sew a B to 2 adjacent edges of D, forming a triangle. Sew the long edge of each triangle to the long edge of each E.

Arrange the squares as shown in the diagram. Join the top and bottom rows by sewing the squares to each side of an F. Sew the remaining F's to each side of G; then join the top and bottom rows with the F-G-F strip to complete the design.

Quilt the block to emphasize the medium and dark patchwork.

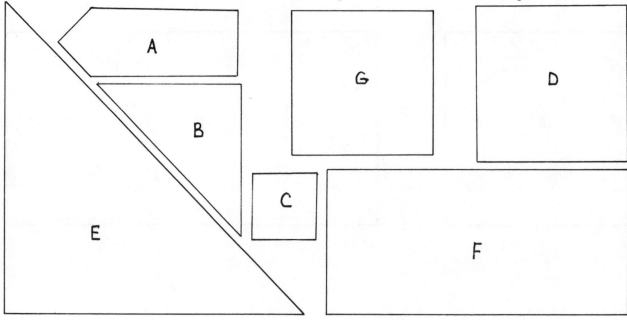

Hopscotch

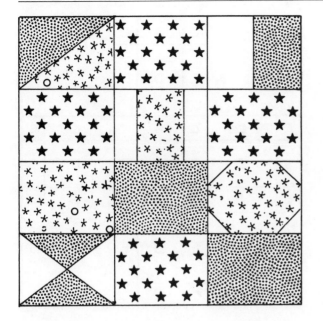

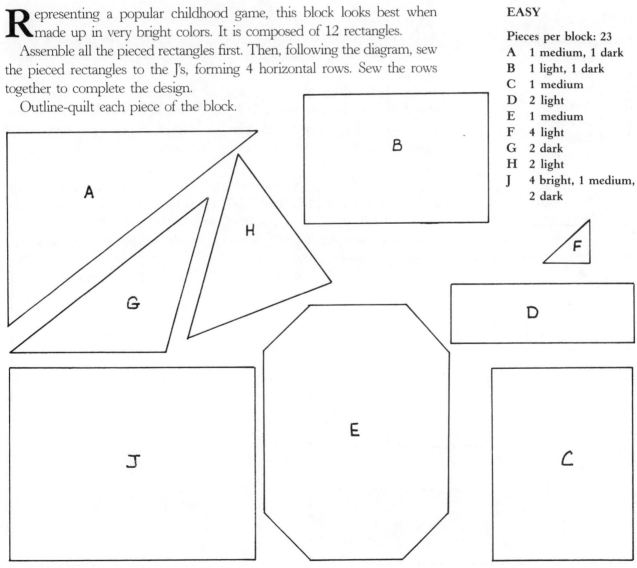

Representing a popular childhood game, this block looks best when made up in very bright colors. It is composed of 12 rectangles.

Assemble all the pieced rectangles first. Then, following the diagram, sew the pieced rectangles to the J's, forming 4 horizontal rows. Sew the rows together to complete the design.

Outline-quilt each piece of the block.

EASY

Pieces per block: 23
A   1 medium, 1 dark
B   1 light, 1 dark
C   1 medium
D   2 light
E   1 medium
F   4 light
G   2 dark
H   2 light
J   4 bright, 1 medium,
    2 dark

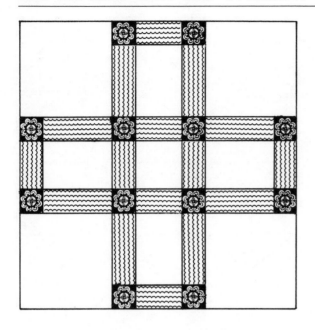

		C	B	C		
	F	E	D	E	F	
C	E	C	B	C	E	C
B	D	B	A	B	D	B
C	E	C	B	C	E	C
	F	E	D	E	F	
		C	B	C		

EASY

Pieces per block: 37

A	1	light
B	8	medium
C	12	dark
D	4	light
E	8	medium
F	4	light

Add a distinctive touch to your sampler quilt with this traditional design that looks like the windows in the game youngsters play. It is especially dramatic when the C squares are cut from a dark fabric. Construct the block in 3 horizontal rows.

Construct the central row first. Sew a B to each side of A. Sew a C to each end of 4 of the same B's. Sew C-B-C to each side of B-A-B. Sew an E to each long edge of 2 D's. Sew the E-D-E's to each side of the completed central square. Complete the strip by sewing the remaining C-B-C strips to each end.

To construct the upper and lower rows, sew a C to each end of 2 B's. Sew an E to each end of 2 D's. Sew C-B-C to E-D-E, forming the central square of each row. Sew an F to each side of them to complete the upper and lower rows. Sew the rows together as shown in the diagram, matching seams carefully, to complete the design.

Quilt the block to emphasize the medium and dark patchwork.

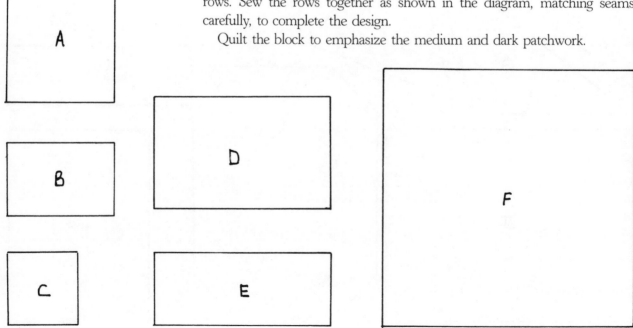

Wooden Blocks

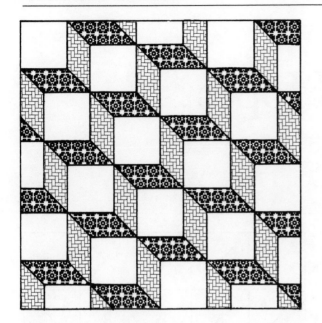

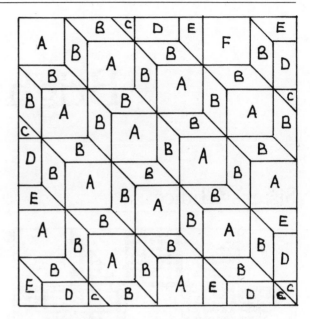

T his block is challenging because the pattern is intricate and many of the pieces must be inset into one another; see How to Inset (page 15). Accurate cutting and piecing are essential for the successful completion of this design.

Following the diagram, sew all medium and dark B's together. Inset an A into each right angle formed by the B's. Sew the A-B blocks together in diagonal strips, sewing each A to a a dark B. Sew the strips together, insetting a medium B at each A-B seam. Fill in the edges with the C, D and E pieces to complete the design.

Outline-quilt each edge of the blocks.

CHALLENGING

Pieces per block: 63

A   15 light
B   15 medium, 15 dark reversed
C   3 medium, 3 dark reversed
D   6 light
E   3 medium, 3 dark reversed

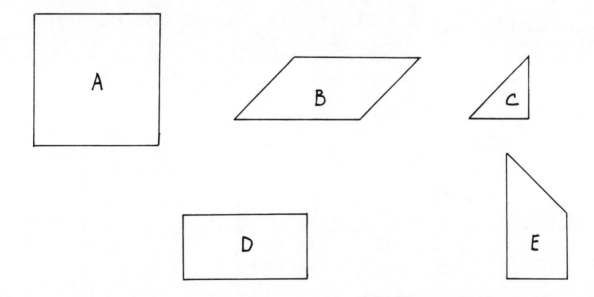

Bright Hopes

Sister's Choice

EASY

Pieces per block: 33
A 8 light, 8 dark
B 8 light, 9 dark

Though simple to construct, this block appears complicated because of the light and dark patterns. It is assembled in 5 horizontal rows.

First, construct all the A squares by sewing a light A to a dark A. Next, arrange all the pieces as shown in the diagram. Sew the squares together to form 5 horizontal strips. Sew the strips together, matching seams carefully, to complete the design.

Outline-quilt the dark pieces.

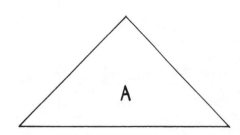

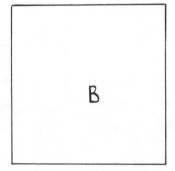

Children of Israel

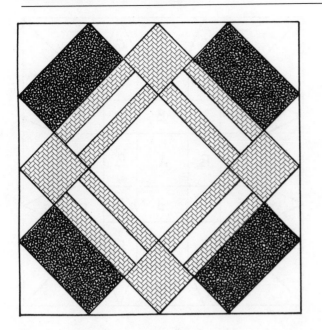

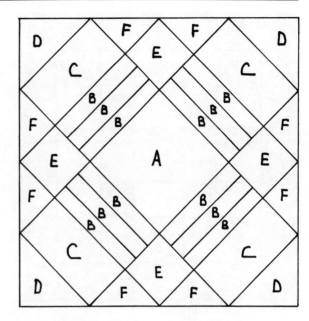

S tudy the block; you'll see that the design can be constructed with 2 large triangles centrally connected by a diagonal strip.

Begin by assembling the central strip. Sew a medium B to each long edge of 2 light B's; sew to opposite sides of A. Sew a C to the B at each end. Sew a D to each C.

Next, construct the triangles. Sew a medium B to each long edge of the remaining light B's. Sew a C to 1 long edge of each of the B rectangles. Sew a D to each C. Sew 2 F's to adjacent edges of each E. Sew the F-E-F triangles to each side of the strips just made as shown in the diagram. Matching seams carefully, sew the pieced triangles to each side of the central strip to complete the design.

Outline-quilt each section of patchwork in the block.

MODERATE

Pieces per block: 33

A	1 light
B	4 light, 8 medium
C	4 dark
D	4 light
E	4 medium
F	8 light

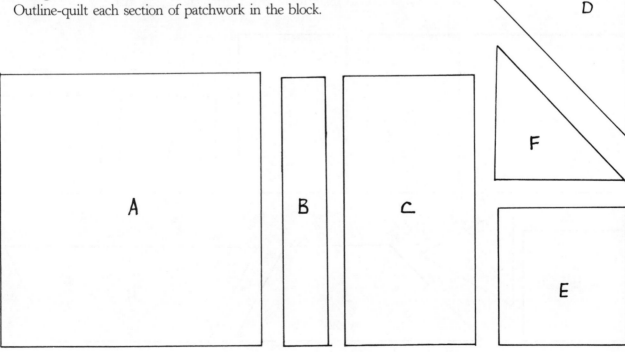

Godmother's Gift

(Color photos, pages B1 and C2)

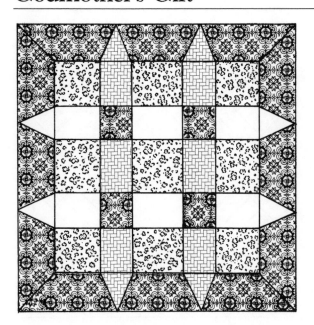

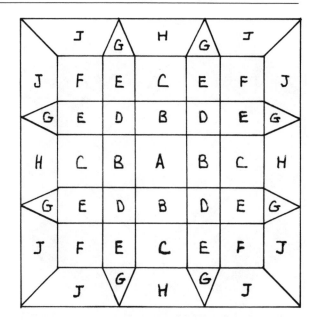

MODERATE

Pieces per block: 45

A	1 medium
B	2 light, 2 bright
C	4 medium
D	4 dark
E	4 light, 4 bright
F	4 medium
G	4 light, 4 bright
H	4 dark
J	4 dark + 4 dark reversed

The pieced central square of this design is bordered by strips of the dark fabric that needs to be mitred at the corners.

Construct the central square first, beginning with the middle strip. Sew a B to each side of A; sew a C to each B. Next, construct the inner strips. Sew a D to each short edge of B; sew an E to each D. Sew to each side of the middle strip. Then construct the adjoining outer strips. Sew an E to each side of C; sew an F to each E. Matching seams carefully, sew the strips just made to each of the inner strips.

For the border, sew a G to each side of H. Sew a J to each G, being sure to use reversed J's on each strip. Sew the border strips to the central square, matching seams carefully. Mitre the corners.

Quilt around the arrow-shaped strips and the border.

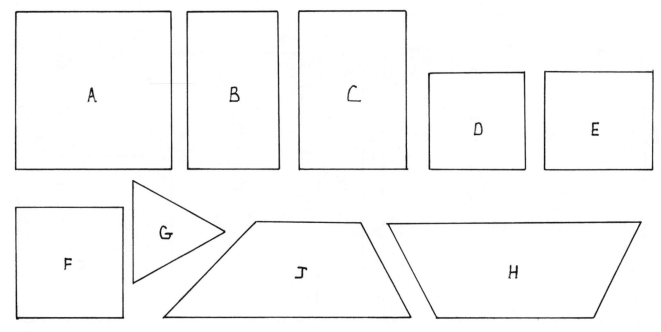

Grandma's Red & White

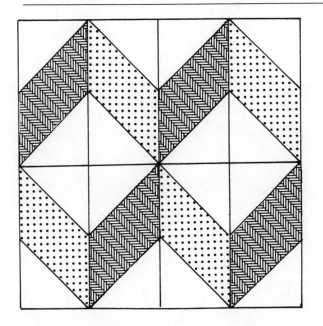
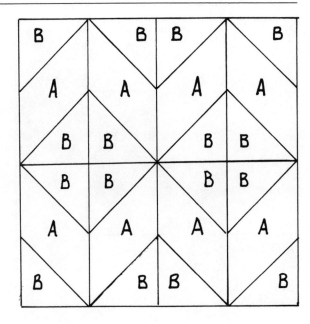

The use of medium and dark fabrics in this striking block gives the design incredible depth; it is composed of 8 pieced rectangles.

Sew a B to each long edge of each A. Arrange the rectangles as shown in the diagram. Join the 4 rectangles in rows, matching seams carefully, to form each half. Sew the halves together to complete the design.

Outline-quilt the medium and dark pieces.

EASY

Pieces per block: 24

A   4 medium, 4 dark
     reversed

B   16 light

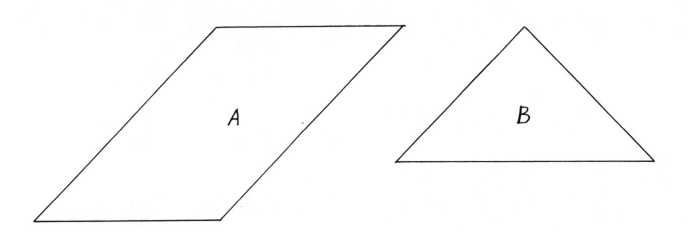

Grandmother's Attic

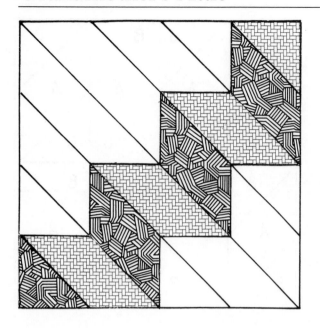

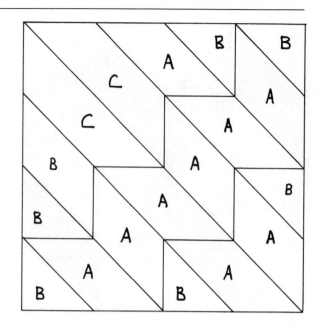

MODERATE

Pieces per block: 18

A   2 light + 2 light reversed,
     3 medium,
     3 dark reversed

B   4 light, 1 medium, 1 dark

C   1 light + 1 light
     reversed

The steps to Grandmother's attic are always fun to climb, especially when the attic is full of boxes. This block is composed of 6 strips (which run diagonally across the block) plus the 2 corner triangles.

Construct each strip by following the diagram. Sew a light A, B or C to each side of each medium and dark A. Sew these strips together, matching seams carefully. Sew the B pieces to each corner to complete the design.

Quilt the block to emphasize the effect of the steps.

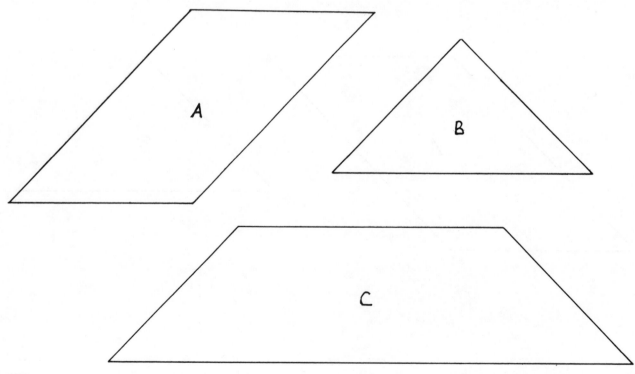

Grandmother's Choice

(Color photo, page B1)

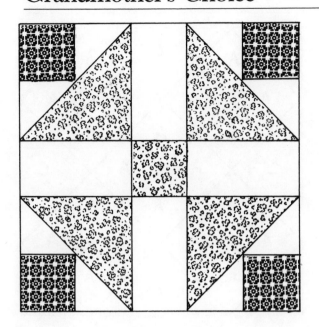

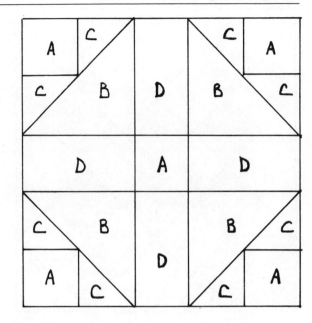

Ⅰn this block, a central cross formed by the A-D pieces joins the 4 pieced corner squares.

Make all the squares the same way. Sew a C to 2 adjacent edges of each dark A. Sew a B to each of the triangles just made to complete the squares. For the top and bottom strips, sew a pieced square to each long edge of 2 D's. Sew a D to each side of the remaining A. Sew the top and bottom strips to each side of D-A-D, matching seams carefully, to complete the design.

Quilt around the medium and dark patchwork.

EASY

Pieces per block: 21

A 1 medium, 4 dark
B 4 medium
C 8 light
D 4 light

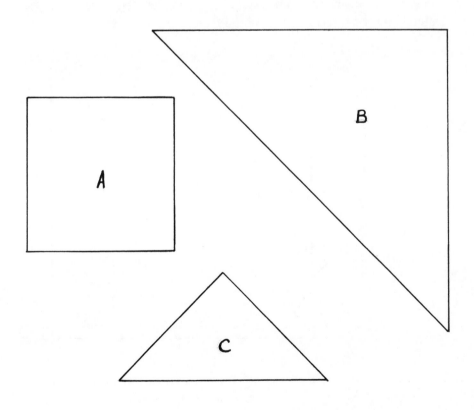

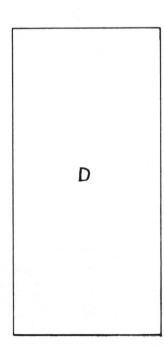

167

Grandmother's Cross

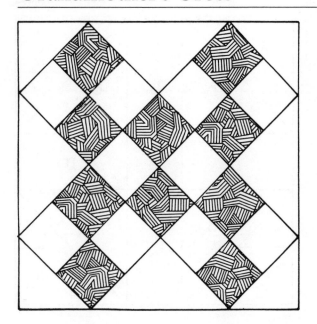

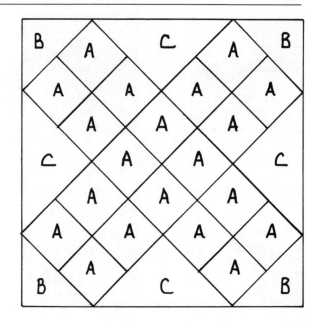

MODERATE

Pieces per block: 28
A   10 light, 10 dark
B   4 light
C   4 light

Matching the seams in the central cross may be tricky, but the finished effect is delightful, especially if highly contrasting fabrics are used. The design is constructed by joining 2 large triangles to a central strip.

Construct the central strip first. Alternating light and dark, sew 6 pairs of light and dark A's together. Sew the pairs together, as shown in the diagram. Sew a B to each end of the pieced C strip.

For the triangles, sew together 4 pairs of light and dark A's. Sew 2 pairs together, making 2 squares. Sew a B to one side of each square. Sew a C to each side of the A-B strip to form 2 triangles. Sew a triangle to each side of the central strip, matching seams carefully, to complete the design.

Outline-quilt each piece in the central cross.

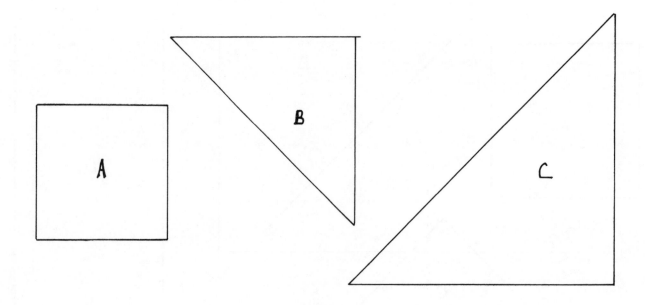

Grandmother's Favorite

(Color photos, pages B1 and B2)

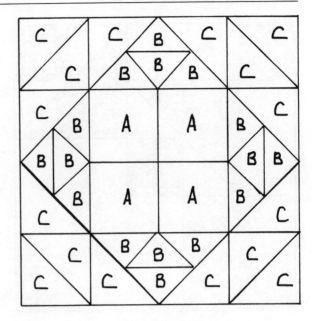

This pretty block produces very different effects, depending upon your choices and placement of light and dark fabrics. It has many pieces, but the construction is easy.

To begin, sew together the 4 A pieces to make the central square. Assemble 4 pieced B triangles following the diagram. Sew 1 to each side of the central square. Construct 4 C triangles as shown in the diagram; sew 1 to each corner to complete the design.

Quilt around the bright and dark pieces.

MODERATE

Pieces per block: 36
A   2 light, 2 bright
B   4 bright, 12 dark
C   10 white, 2 light, 4 dark

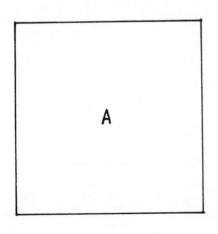

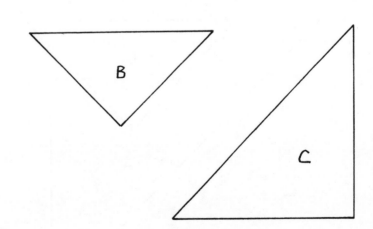

Grandmother's Puzzle

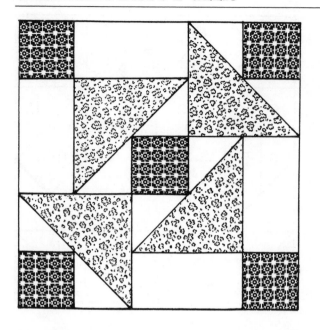

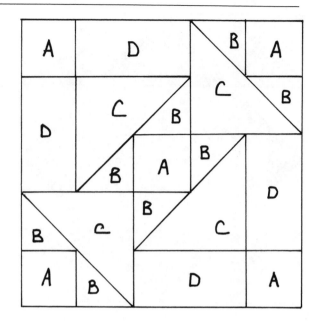

CHALLENGING

Pieces per block: 21

A 5 dark
B 8 light
C 4 medium
D 4 light

Why is this block called a puzzle? It's a bit tricky to assemble! Study the block carefully; you'll see that it comprises 1 large square (top left), 2 small squares (top right, bottom left) and a partial square (bottom right).

Begin with the large square. Sew a B to 2 adjacent edges of an A. Sew a C to the triangle just made, then sew a D to an edge of the C. Sew an A to a D. Sew A-D to the other edge of C as shown in the diagram. For each small square, sew a B to 2 adjacent edges of an A. Sew a C to the rectangle just made.

Arrange the pieced squares and the remaining pieces as shown in the diagram. Sew the remaining B's to adjacent edges of the central A. Sew a C to B-B. Sew a D to the side of C. Sew the remaining A and D pieces together, then sew to the bottom of C. Inset the small squares into each corner to complete the design.

Quilt around the medium and dark patchwork.

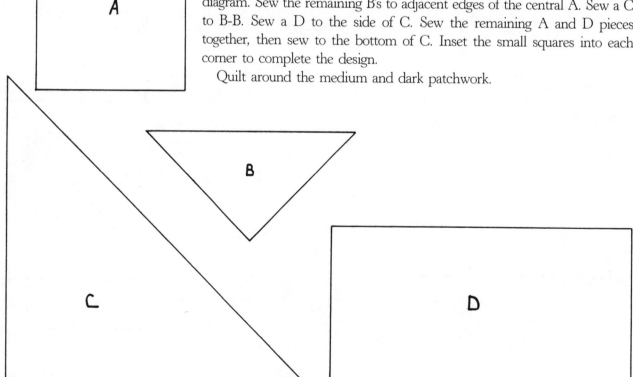

Child of Mine

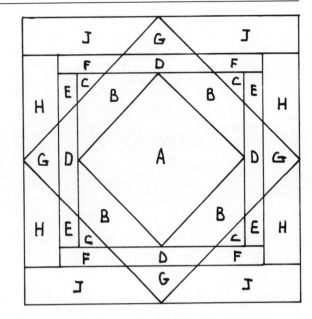

This lovely design is constructed in concentric squares that turn and expand. The patchwork makes them appear like octagons.

To begin, sew the long edge of each B to A. Sew a C to each B, forming a central square. For the next section of patchwork, following the diagram and using reversed pieces where necessary, sew an E to each short edge of 2 D's; sew an F to each short edge of the remaining 2 D's. Sew E-D-E to each side, then sew F-D-F to the top and bottom of the central square.

For the outer section, sew an H to each short edge of 2 G's; sew a J to each short edge of the remaining 2 G's. Sew H-G-H to each side of the central section. Sew J-G-J to the top and bottom to complete the design.

Outline-quilt the medium and dark pieces.

MODERATE

Pieces per block: 33

A   1 medium
B   4 bright
C   4 light
D   4 light
E   2 dark + 2 dark reversed
F   2 dark + 2 dark reversed
G   4 dark
H   2 bright + 2 bright reversed
J   2 bright + 2 bright reversed

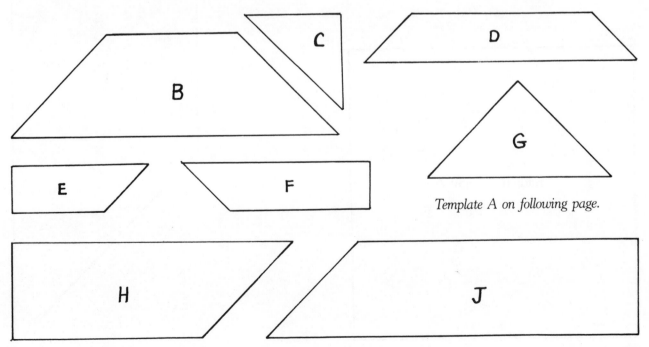

Template A on following page.

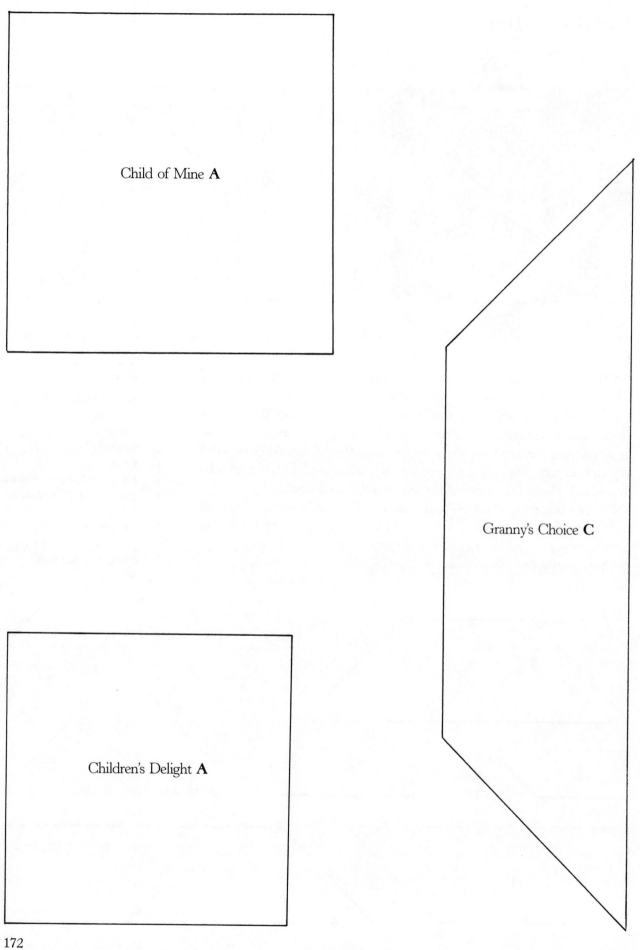

Child of Mine **A**

Granny's Choice **C**

Children's Delight **A**

Granny's Choice

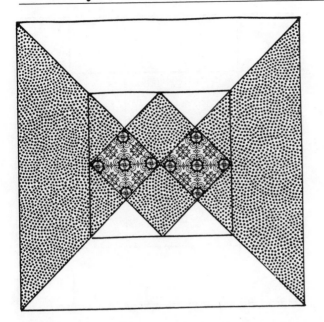

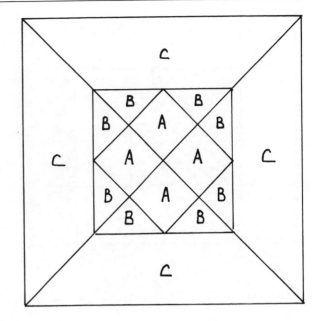

S imple to sew, this block is composed of 4 triangles. You must be careful to match the seams in the middle.

To make each triangle, sew 2 B's to adjacent edges of each A following the diagram for placement of color. Sew a C to each B-B edge. Next, sew 2 pairs of the triangles together, making each half of the design. Sew the halves together, matching seams carefully, to complete the design.

Quilt the central A pieces to echo the diamond shape, forming concentric diamonds across the block.

EASY

Pieces per block: 16
A   2 medium, 2 dark
B   4 light, 4 dark
C   2 light, 2 dark

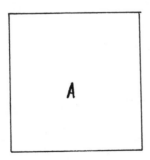

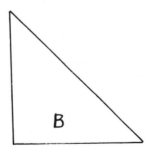

Template C on facing page.

Children's Delight

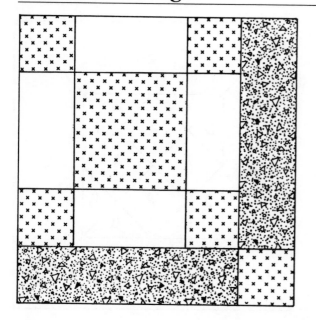

EASY

Pieces per block: 12

A 1 medium
B 4 light
C 5 medium
D 2 dark

This is an excellent block for beginners because it is so quick and easy to make. Study the block; you'll see that it is composed of an A-B-C square bordered on 2 sides by D strips and a C square.

First, assemble the A-B-C square. Sew a B to each side of A; sew a C to each short edge of the remaining B's. Sew the rows together, matching seams carefully. Sew a D to the right side of the square. Sew a C to the remaining D; sew D-C to the bottom edge to complete the design.

Quilt around the medium and dark patchwork.

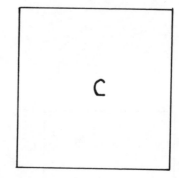

Template A on page 172.

Mommy's Favorite

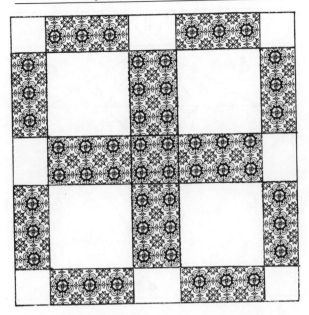

F	E	C	E	F
E	D	B	D	E
C	B	A	B	C
E	D	B	D	E
F	E	C	E	F

The most appealing designs are sometimes very simple—yet dramatic—such as this one. It is easily constructed in 5 horizontal strips.

Construct the central strip first. Sew a B to each side of A; sew a C to each B. Next, make the inner strips by sewing a D to each long edge of the remaining B's; sew an E to each D. Sew these strips to each side of the central strip, matching seams carefully.

Finally, construct the outer strips. Sew an E to each side of C; sew an F to each E. Sew the completed outer strips to the pieced central section to complete the design.

Quilt the block in concentric diamonds. Or echo the squares, outlining each square, then quilting 1 or 2 squares in the middle of each.

EASY

Pieces per block: 25
A   1 dark
B   4 dark
C   4 light
D   4 light
E   8 dark
F   4 light

A

B

C

F

D

E

Mother's Child

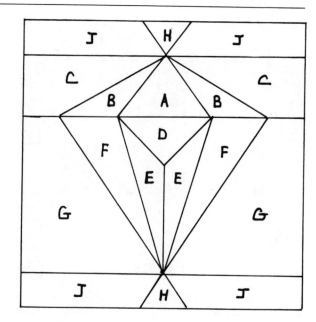

CHALLENGING

Pieces per block: 18

A   1 light
B   1 medium + 1 medium reversed
C   1 dark + 1 dark reversed
D   1 light
E   1 medium + 1 medium reversed
F   1 light + 1 light reversed
G   1 dark + 1 dark reversed
H   2 dark
J   2 light + 2 light reversed

This unusual design slightly resembles a cut diamond. It has tricky angles and points to sew, but if marked and cut accurately, shouldn't present too much difficulty. Construct it in 4 horizontal strips.

First, sew a B to each side of A; sew a C to each B. Sew the E's together, then inset D into the angle made; see How to Inset (page 15). Sew an F to each E; sew a G to each F. Sew together the 2 strips just made, matching seams carefully.

For the top and bottom strips, sew a J to each side of each H, being sure to use reversed pieces on each strip. Sew to the top and bottom of the block, matching points, to complete the design.

Outline-quilt the diamond, repeating the shape across the rest of the block.

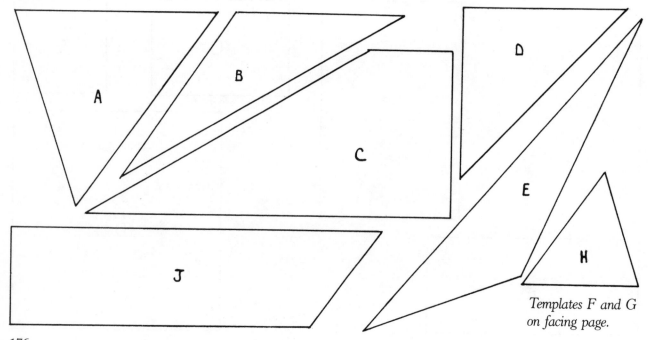

Templates F and G on facing page.

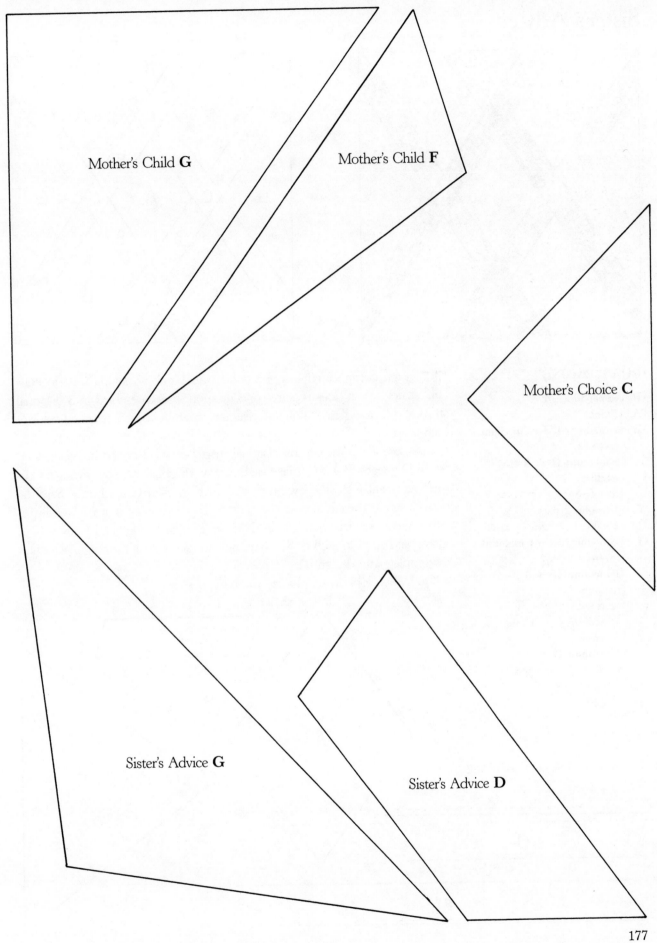

Mother's Child **G**

Mother's Child **F**

Mother's Choice **C**

Sister's Advice **G**

Sister's Advice **D**

Sister's Advice

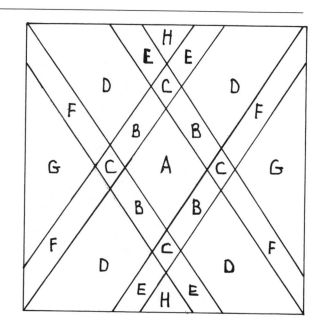

CHALLENGING

Pieces per block: 25
- **A** 1 light
- **B** 1 medium I + 1 medium I reversed,
  1 medium II + 1 medium II reversed
- **C** 2 bright, 2 dark
- **D** 2 light + 2 light reversed
- **E** 1 medium I + 1 medium I reversed,
  1 medium II + 1 medium II reversed
- **F** 1 medium I + 1 medium I reversed,
  1 medium II + 1 medium II reversed
- **G** 2 light
- **H** 2 light

Templates D and G on preceding page.

Though complicated in appearance, this block is not difficult to construct, but it does require concentration. It is assembled in 3 diagonal strips and 2 triangles. Follow the diagram carefully for position and color of each strip.

First, construct the central diagonal strip. Sew a B to opposite edges of A. Sew a D to each B. Next, make each narrow diagonal strip by sewing a C to each short end of a B. Sew an E and an F to each C as shown. Sew the narrow strips to each side of the central strip, matching seams carefully.

To make each triangle, sew an E and an F to each side of a D. Sew a G to each F and an H to each E. Sew a triangle to each side of the diagonal section to complete the design.

Quilt the block to emphasize the narrow strips.

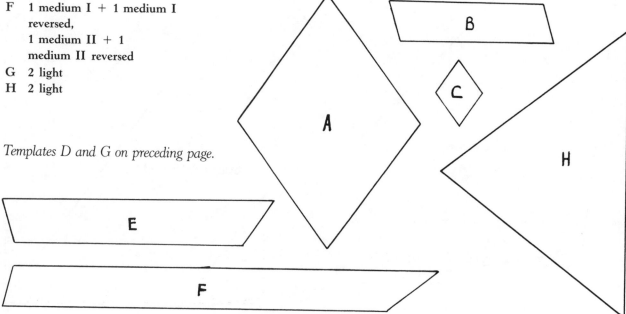

Mother's Choice

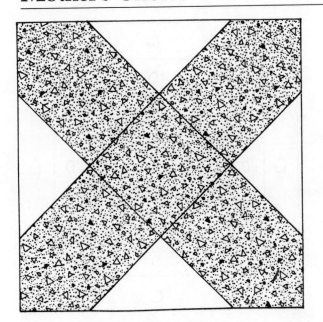

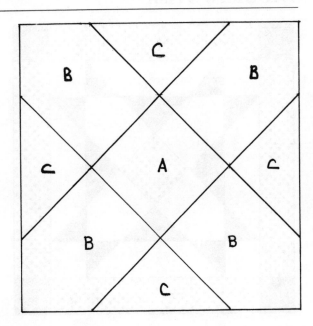

Composed of 2 triangles sewn to each side of a diagonal strip, this design is easy to construct. It is also very quick to make because there are only 9 large pieces.

First, make the diagonal strip. Sew a B to each side of A. To make each of the 2 triangles, sew a C to each side of a B as shown in the diagram. Sew a triangle to each side of the diagonal strip to complete the design.

Quilt the block to emphasize the cross.

EASY

Pieces per block: 9
A   1 dark
B   4 dark
C   4 light

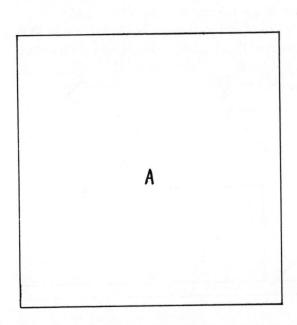

Template C on page 177.

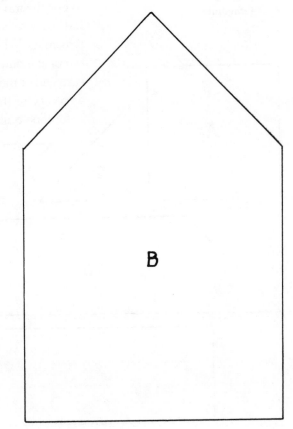

Mother's Wish

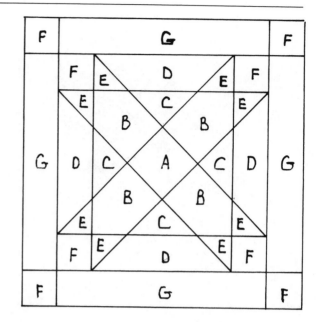

MODERATE

Pieces per block: 33

A 1 medium
B 4 light
C 4 dark
D 4 light
E 8 dark
F 4 light, 4 dark
G 4 medium

Construct this block in 3 steps. First, make the central square, which is composed of 2 right-angled triangles sewn to each side of a diagonal strip. Then construct the inner and outer borders and sew them to the central square.

To make the central square, construct the diagonal strip first. Sew a B to each side of A. To make each triangle, sew a C to each long edge of B. Sew a C-B-C to each side of B-A-B to complete the central square.

For the inner border, sew an E to each angled edge of each D. Sew an E-D-E strip to each side of the central square. Sew a light F to each end of the remaining E-D-E strips; sew to the top and bottom of the middle.

For the outer border, sew a G to each side of the block. Sew a dark D to each end of the remaining G's. Sew F-G-F to the top and bottom of the block to complete the design.

Outline-quilt the dark pieces.

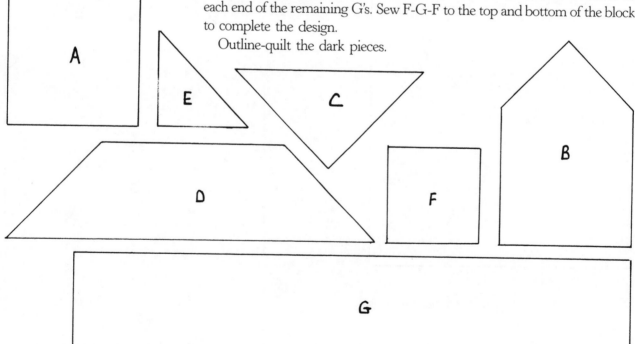

Mother's Dream

(Color photos, pages B1 and C1)

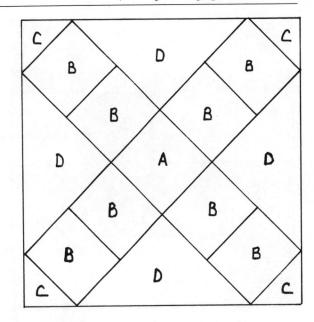

This appealing block is composed of 2 large triangles, connected by a pieced central strip.

Construct the central strip first. Sew a dark B to each side of A. Sew a light B to each dark B. Sew a C to each end to complete the central strip. For each triangle, sew a light B to a dark B. Sew a C to each light B. Sew a D to each side of B-B-C as shown in the diagram. Sew a triangle to each side of the central strip to complete the design.

Quilt the block to emphasize the central cross.

EASY

Pieces per block: 17
A 1 light
B 4 light, 4 dark
C 4 medium
D 4 medium

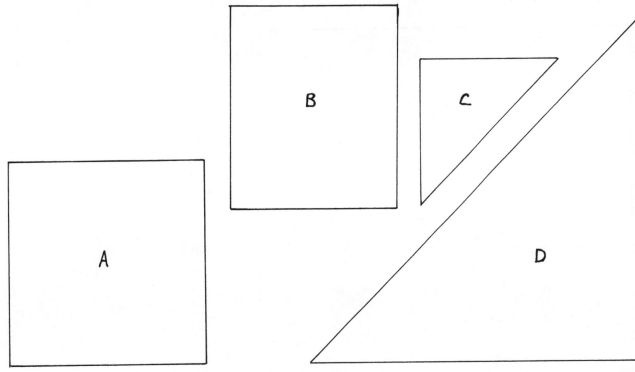

Pride & Joy

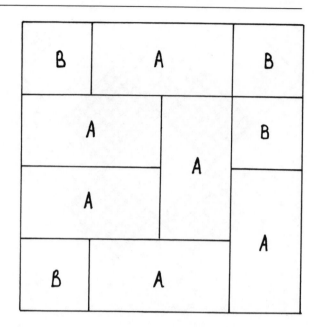

EASY

Pieces per block: 10
A 2 light, 3 medium, 1 dark
B 1 light, 3 dark

An excellent choice for beginners, this unusual design is very simple to make.

Construct the top strip first by sewing a dark B to each short end of a medium A. Next, construct the square on the lower left side of the block. Sew a light A to a medium A; sew a dark A to the square just made. Sew a dark B to a light A; sew to the base of the A-A strip.

To complete the design, sew a light B to a medium A; sew to the right side of the square. Sew the top strip to the bottom.

When quilting, ignore the seams; quilt in a circular or shell pattern across the entire block.

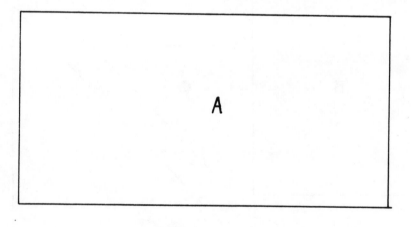

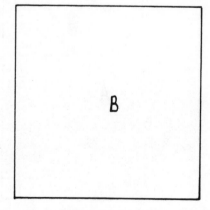

Mother's Delight

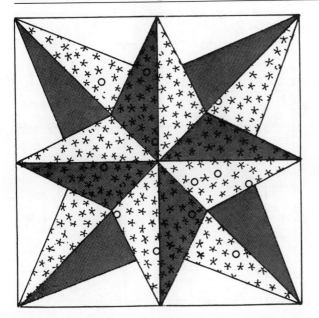

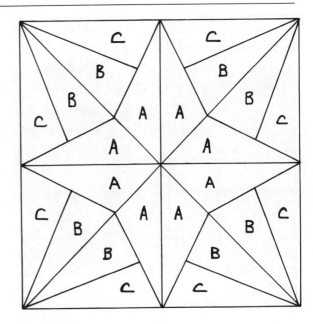

Very deceiving, this design appears quite difficult. But if you study the block closely, you'll see that it is composed of 4 pieced triangles.

To make each triangle, sew a bright and dark A together. Next, sew a bright and medium B each to a C. Sew the triangles just made to A-A as shown in the diagram. Sew the 4 triangles together, matching seams carefully, to complete the design.

Outline-quilt each piece of the block.

MODERATE

Pieces per block: 24
A   4 bright, 4 dark reversed
B   4 bright, 4 medium
    reversed
C   4 light + 4 light reversed

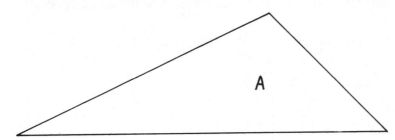

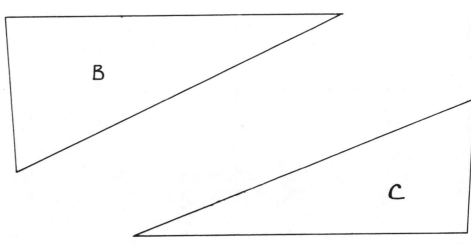

Bright Hopes

(Color photo, page B1)

MODERATE

Pieces per block: 20
A   4 dark
B   4 white, 4 light, 4 bright,
    4 medium

This design is composed of 4 squares, each constructed in the same manner.

Sew each B strip to A in a clockwise direction beginning with the top strip; the left end of the first B will be unstitched until the last stage of stitching the strips. To sew the fourth B strip to A, turn the stitching sharply to join it to the first B. Repeat for the other 3 sections of the block, following the diagram carefully. Arrange the 4 sections as shown in the diagram; sew 2 quarters together to form each half of the block. Sew the halves together to complete the design.

Quilt around each A piece and the outer edges of the B strips.

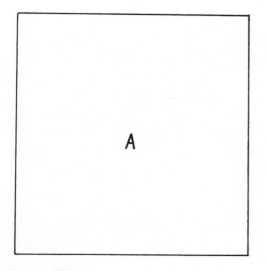

Wishing & Hoping

(Color photo, page B1)

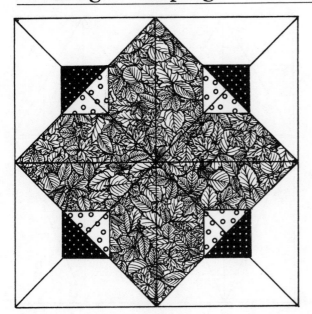
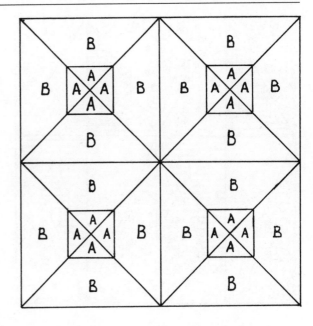

The placement of light and medium fabrics creates the impression of a diamond superimposed on a square. This block actually is assembled by joining 4 identical squares.

Construct each square the same way. Sew a medium B to each bright A. Sew a light B to each dark A. Sew the bright A/medium B triangles together to form half of the square. Sew the dark A/light B triangles together to form the other half of the square. Sew the halves together, matching seams carefully, to complete each square.

Sew 2 pairs of squares together, along the medium B edges, for each half of the design. Sew the halves together, also along the medium B edges, to complete the design.

Quilt close to each seam of the patchwork.

EASY

Pieces per block: 32
A   8 bright, 8 dark
B   8 light, 8 medium

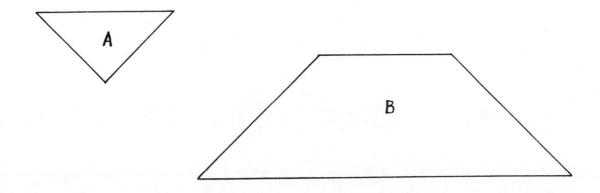

Twins

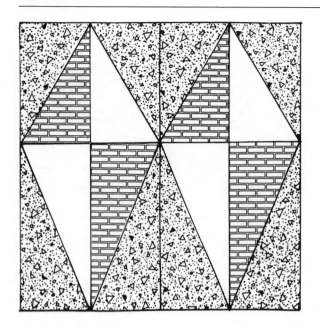
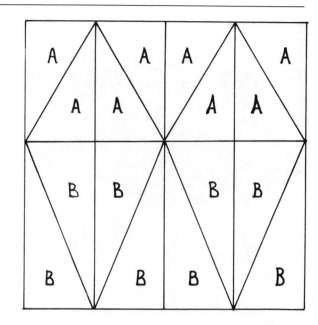

EASY

Pieces per block: 16

A   2 light, 2 bright reversed,
     2 medium + 2 medium
     reversed

B   2 light reversed, 2 bright,
     2 medium + 2 medium
     reversed

This design is easily constructed in 2 vertical sections, each assembled in an identical way.

Sew each light A to a bright A and each light B to a bright B. Sew the A-A and B-B triangles together, matching seams. Sew medium A's and B's around each pieced diamond as shown in the diagram. Sew the 2 rectangles together to complete the design.

Quilt concentric diamonds, starting at the middle of each "twin" and working out towards the edges until the lines begin to intersect.

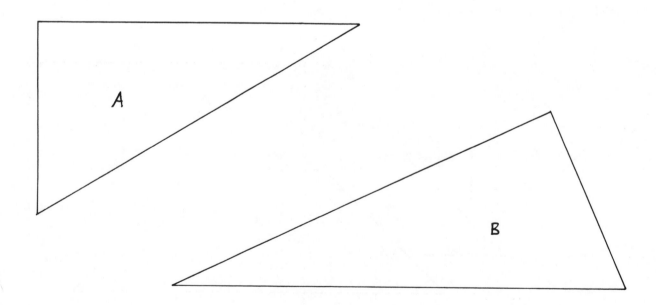

Bundle of Joy

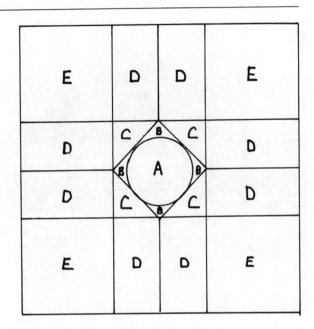

The central square is the challenging part of this block. After that, it's all straight and simple sewing. See Sewing Curves (page 16).

To begin, sew the B's around A to make a square; sew a C to each B-B edge to complete the central square. Sew 4 pairs of D's together at the long edges. Sew a pair of D's to each side of the central square. Sew an E to each side of the remaining D pairs. Sew the E-D-D-E strips to the top and bottom of the central strip, matching seams carefully, to complete the design.

Quilt the block in concentric circles.

CHALLENGING

Pieces per block: 21
A   1 dark
B   4 light
C   4 medium
D   8 light
E   4 medium

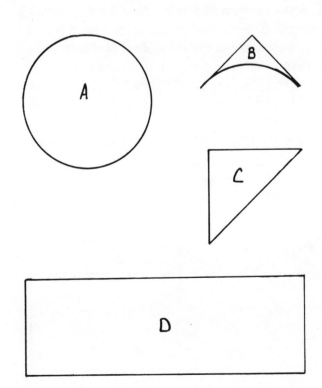

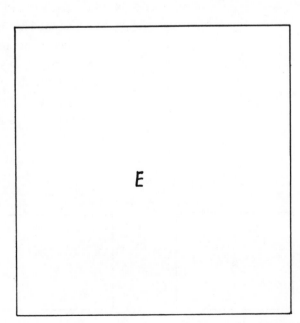

Grandma's House

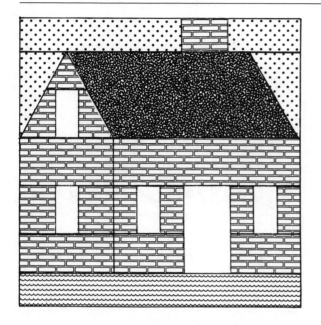

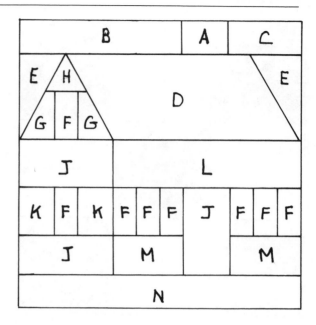

MODERATE

Pieces per block: 26

A	1 medium
B	1 light
C	1 light
D	1 dark reversed
E	1 light + 1 light reversed
F	4 white, 4 medium
G	1 medium + 1 medium reversed
H	1 medium
J	1 white, 2 medium
K	2 medium
L	1 medium
M	2 medium
N	1 bright

This charming design will probably be a favorite for most children, who always love to go to Grandma's house. For fun, add some decorative touches with embroidery such as a doorknob, the house number, windowpanes, and flowers growing around the base of the house.

The block is assembled in 4 horizontal strips—the chimney, roof, house and grass strips. For the chimney strip, sew B and C to each side of A. For the roof strip, sew an E to the right edge of D. Sew a G to each side of a white F; sew H to the top. Sew G-H to the left edge of D. Sew the remaining E to G-H to complete the roof strip.

For the house strip, sew a K to each side of a white F; sew a medium J to each long edge of K-F-K. Sew a medium F to each side of the 2 remaining white F's; sew an M to each F-F-F. Sew the pieces just made to each side of the white J as shown in the diagram; sew L to the top of the piece just made. Sew the left and right sections together to complete the house strip.

Sew the chimney and roof strips together. Sew the roof and house strips together, matching seams carefully. Sew the house to the grass strip (N) to complete the design.

Quilt the block to define the outline of the house, including the roof, windows and door.

Quilt vertical lines on N piece to simulate grass.

A

B

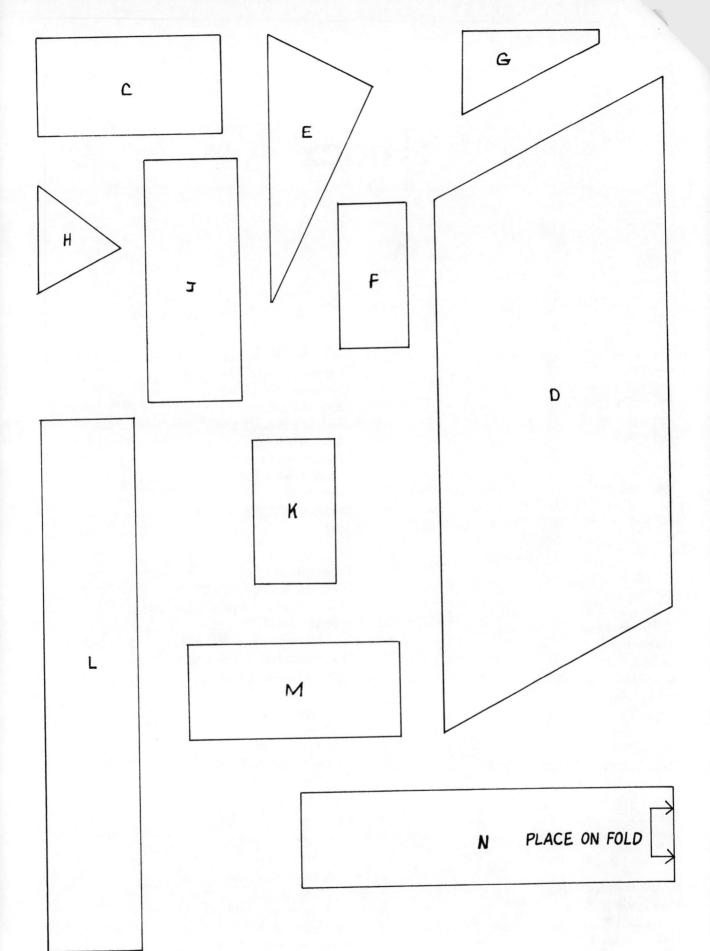

C

E

G

H

J

F

D

K

L

M

N   PLACE ON FOLD

Index

About the Author

Linda Macho Seward has been an active needleworker since she could hold a needle. She graduated with honors from Tobe-Coburn School for Fashion Careers and has a B.S. degree in home economics from Douglass College, Rutgers University. Linda, who has written several books, including one on quilting, is also a needlework designer. Many of her designs have been published in needlework magazines. During her career, she has edited many needlework and crafts books and now lives in London with her husband where she spends a great deal of time at her typewriter and quilting frame.